Two

Voices

The Non-Logician

Tim Snavely

A Non-Prophet Organization

Two Voices

Contents

Introduction

There are two voices inside my head, and they are both my own. I call them Zero and One. One spoke as me first, as that inquisitive inner voice that naturally drives me to action in pursuit of meaning. One asked questions like "What's this?" "Who are you?" "When's dinner?" "How does this work?" and "Why should I, mommy?" One explores the world, relying on appearances and predetermined explanations to build a schematic interpretation of reality. Although I'm not certain, I'm reasonably confident that everybody alive has a One inside their minds with varying degrees of vigor and gullibility to be satisfied with the conclusions reached. One is, in many regards, life itself, because without it, questions like "Is this an invitation for sex?" or "Why is my hand on fire?" would never be asked. Life would die out very quickly, whenever and wherever cognition plays a major role in the organism.

Not everybody has a Zero, though. But I may be wrong. Among those with an inner Zero voice, however cynical or absurd its questions are spoken, its end goal of death is clear, even if it's not death itself. Zero brings death to nonsensical and incomplete ideas and is also disagreeable for the sake of erring on the side of caution lest an idea be filled with error itself. Zero's questions sound like, "How is this not that?" "Why even bother?" "Do I even want dinner?" and "What is the meaning of meaning?" This last question in particular is an absolute wrecking ball if Zero's madness was never kept in check by One's ability to implode the question and sometimes even provide a satisfactory answer to silence Zero for a while.

My Zero and One are at peace, always engaging in a playful civil war, the battles are a fun game for me. They agree that they are after the same goal, and that both the complete domination of One over Zero or Zero over One would make the goal much harder to reach. One's victory would claim to have found something when it had actually not, and Zero's victory would be self-refuting, bittersweet, while still ending up nowhere closer to the goal of an objective meaning of meaning itself. And so they constantly scrimmage, in hopes of achieving a mere fragment of the goal together, so they could share the glory of irrefutable meaning to all who saw it.

Before giving these *Two Voices* dialogue in a Socratic debate that will last for three fictional days, I shall remind the reader that both of these voices are mine. Some of you may relate more with One, who is more hopeful, optimistic, and forgiving of minor discrepancies by providing a benefit of the doubt towards Zero and other Ones and Zeros. Some of you may relate more with Zero, who is more calculating, realistic, pessimistic, skeptical, and relentless when any perceived imperfection comes into view. One's victory often leads to gullible ignorance and premature satisfaction. Zero's victory typically leads to self-loathing and the loneliness that comes with going against the crowd. May the weaker of these *Two Voices* grow in you to either humble your pride or to esteem your low self-esteem.

Day 1: The World

One: Alright Zero, I reckon today will be the day we figure things out! It's such a beautiful day; just look at this large imaginary field we can play in.

Zero: There's nothing here besides us, One. Such a dreary landscape, I'd say. But those are merely our opinions and add nothing to the discussion anyway, save that we grant there to be a medium of sorts for us to engage in discourse.

One: Do you see what I see? A grassy plain with the occasional tree and a high afternoon sun, pleasantly covered at the moment by the sparse clouds?

Zero: No, actually. I see a uniformly gray space occupied by us. I'm just a dark shadowy humanoid figure, and you're a bright light humanoid figure, expressing yourself like a car's headlight in the fog. Rather poetic, like a couple of lone chess pieces destined to stalemate.

One: Incredible! Two settings, yet one medium. I must say that there appear to be a couple more things we may agree on. I, too, see you as a black knight figure, and myself as a white knight, although with much crisper detail. Who our respective kings are, I'm not sure, and I'm not sure if it matters. So may we agree that there is a common medium, we are contrasted by darkness and light, and that we are about to contest in a battle of sorts?

Zero: The battle has already begun! White moved first!

One: Yes, it appears I did. Remind me now, Zero, why can't you go first?

Zero: Perhaps I did, out in the real world. *Whatever that means.* But here in this concept space, it isn't exactly fitting for my skeptical doubt to be moved until I see something suspiciously out of order.

One: I suppose… I'm not here to discuss Nothing, since we had that battle last week. I should congratulate you, Zero, for that clever move that negated the medium itself made me immobile, and allowed you to move freely in the void.

Zero: Thank you, One. But I shall admit that going nowhere is rather dull. A cheap party trick, sure, but unhelpful in confronting the existential issues we both seek to resolve. Personally, I'd love to have answered these questions to my full satisfaction. So for this battle, I'd like to propose a fourth agreement, namely, that there is nothing underlying this concept space medium, and it is just as it is, and no more.

One: A necessary handicap, I agree.

Zero: So then, here is my first question. What do we mean by "medium?"

One: Is it not the world around us? This particular peculiar universe we find ourselves in?

Zero: Likely, but it is a peculiar world indeed. By appearances alone, it seems that we are in two different worlds. The only appearance our worlds hold in common is the general intensity of contrast seen in our entities. Could this commonality be a mere coincidence?

One: More likely, it was because our worlds originated by a mutual designer or designers.

Zero: Oy oy, easy there Sparky. Remember, we agreed that there is nothing underlying this concept space medium. And any mention of world designers would be appealing to an underlying thing. It just is what it is. *But what is it?*

One: Now hold on, doesn't a concept space imply a thinker? And thus imply an intellect capable of designing such a curious world?

Zero: Yes, I think you're right. Reason itself must be the basis for a concept space.

One: I then propose a superior question back to you Zero than asking what this world is. Is there a need to distinguish this concept space from the conscious awareness that is itself thinking about this peculiar concept space?

Zero: If there exist other reasoning entities out in the real world, *whatever that means*, it may be important to distinguish the two, since they would likely reflect on the parallels from here to the real world. If we don't distinguish the thinker from the world here, wouldn't real thinkers in the real world have difficulty distinguishing themselves from the world?

One: You've got a good point. You know what? If we succeed, we'd have a pretty good case against solipsism.

Zero: You have your work cut out for you, One. Distinguish the medium of the self, from the medium of our perplexing concept spaces, and from the medium of the real world.

One: Hmmm, if I were to propose such a distinction on the top of my head, I'd say that the self consists of pure subjectivity, the real world consists of pure objectivity, and these concept spaces may be an impure blend between object and subject.

Zero: Perhaps. But is it possible that our perceptions of the purely objective are tainted by our subject?

One: Inevitably, since the full picture is often obscured.

Zero: Then perhaps we got a bit ahead of ourselves. Although I doubt we could have arrived here any sooner. Since the self is fundamentally subject, which I'll grant for now, and the worlds of interest contain objects in them, distinguish the false self-imagined and therefore subjective objects from the real, true, and objective objects.

One: Wouldn't there be only two factors of concern here? For one, real objects can only be known through our imperfect senses, never purely imagined and self-originated like in the case of a schizophrenic, and they hold some indication of a measurable consistency. The imagined object is bound within the subject until its representation is placed on a real object, where others can judge it as either art or delusions. Even though imagined objects can be fixed to represent real objects, are themselves not bound to the laws of measurable consistency.

Zero: It would seem so. If we acknowledge that sensing a real object may be flawed from the beginning, but define it as being a genuine object beyond the self that doesn't disappear from the world when it goes unobserved…sounds kind of good. But then, how could we determine a genuine subject beyond the self from a false subject? Aren't subjects themselves unbounded by laws of measurable consistency?

One: Subjects are rather flexible and often contradictory, aren't they? Much like our relative concepts spaces.

Zero: A formidable analogy, indeed.

One: It seems the only way to determine a true subject beyond itself would be by connecting it back to its representative true object or objects as we defined them earlier.

Zero: But doing so would require it occurring in this concept space since you noted that it is there where this impure blend between object and subject happens.

One: My subject, yes, but not other subjects.

Zero: Now hold on! You said, and I quote, *"The real world consists of pure objectivity."* I take that to mean that there is no subjectivity in the real world and therefore, no subjects. Any perceived subjects, perhaps including my own, in the real world, mind you, would simply be a misattribution of our object's imperfect senses, to prescribe a subject where there were only ever objects to begin with!

One: I am floored, Zero. So pure subjectivity doesn't even exist? Is it simply an imperfect abstraction of the object?

Zero: Perhaps. But I also add the possibility of subjectivity being an *active* abstraction. So it may exist as such.

One: Thanks for the assist.

Zero: Don't mention it. This fight isn't to the death. But you should still be floored, One. This entails that the self, as subject, is merely an active and imperfect abstraction. And since our perplexing concept space is admittedly tainted by subjectivity, there appears to be nothing to validly distinguish the self from this concept space. We have already seen where this line of reasoning leads, right?

One: It ends with me lying with my back on the floor. So my only option for now is to define objectivity with such eloquent precision so that reality can be distinguished from abstractions.

Zero: I think there lies the problem.

One: What's that? Already striking before I speak?

Zero: Of course! How do you expect to reach an objective meaning of objectivity by using words? Are not words subjective placeholders for the objective things they represent, and not the objective things themselves?

One: Hmmm, I see your point. Describing an object with an abstraction rather than with the object itself. An impossible feat, you're right. Perhaps I should clarify. The abstractions in the form of words used to define meaning will be precise when the objective things themselves are intelligibly distinguishable from the intellect and the abstractions that define them therein.

Zero: It's still a little rough for a methodological definition, but I'll grant it to see how you'll use it.

One: An example of applying this definition is first in order. You know what a word is, right?

Zero: I know one when I observe it, yes.

One: And the word 'word' is a word, I'm sure you do not doubt.

Zero: In this particular context, yes it is.

One: What do you mean, "In this particular context?" Do you imply that the 'word' in question could not be a word in another context?

Zero: Well, yeah. The word 'word' is itself a word, but it's not the word in-itself. *The word 'words' is perhaps closer to the word in-itself, beyond all contexts.* Yet even more precisely, the word 'words' spoken and read in every intelligible language at once would be the most precise word in-itself.

One: I couldn't have said it better, Zero! I'd even add that the intelligibility of a word is vital for the word 'words' being a word. And yet, did you notice? It is not the intelligibility of the word 'words' that makes it the adequate representation of a word in-itself, but the imagined totality of possible intelligible iterations of the word 'words' that would make 'words' an acceptable word in-itself.

Zero: Hmmm, so it seems. This is pretty good. And yet…

One: What?

Zero: Such an iteration does not and could not exist in the real world. It would look and sound like complete garbled nonsense, which renders it meaningless again. So such an iteration must be left as an imagined abstraction to be validly maintained.

One: That should be fine for what I was initially doing. Remember, the current goal is to define objective things with abstractions, not turning the abstractions into objective things. This digression was to begin using the tool you granted me to use.

Zero: Wouldn't the same issue emerge, but going in reverse?

One: I don't understand.

Zero: Alright, for example, you said you see trees in your concept space, correct?

One: Yes, there are a small handful in view. One is right here!

Zero: Great. Walk towards and touch the nearest tree in your concept space. I'll follow your entity's light.

One: Just a few steps away… right here.

Zero: Interesting. You say it is, yet I don't see it. I wonder what happens if I move to stand where your hand is… Nothing here. I can still interact with you like normal. But what do you observe?

One: Zero, you demon! You ghost! How can you walk through the tree like it is nothing, yet the tree resists me? Such a contradictory sensation, feeling both you and the tree at the exact same time in precisely the same space.

Zero: I realized a while ago that you've added some unnecessary logical constraints to your imagination. My concept space is as minimalistic as possible. Even though we both know this imaginary tree isn't here, you chose to interact with it as if it were a real tree.

One: Perhaps conceptual objects can only be simulated to reflect real objects precisely when we choose to put up logical constraints consistent with how they appear to behave in reality.

Zero: Fair enough. So, which constraints do you propose we adhere to? I should probably ask, before allowing this particular tree to be as it is for you, so I can see it in my world as clearly as yours.

One: Our common medium should follow the laws of physics as far as we understand them; and chemistry as well. Solids will be solid, gasses will be gassy, and liquids will be transitional between the two. My solids, like this tree, cannot be your gasses or liquids.

Zero: Okay, okay, fine. I'll allow you to verbally paint this tree here so that our common medium can appear more similar than different. So what attributes do our concept spaces and the real world have in common? If we do this well, constructing our spaces to match each other and reality may be easier, and make our goals achievable as well.

One: We're going all over the place, just to lay down the bedrock fundamentals of the world. So may I now, at last, begin eloquently describing what these three worlds hold in common, not to distinguish the real from the conceptual, but to ensure that the conceptual reflects the real?

Zero: A consensus between our vastly different outlooks is indeed called for. What do you propose this common ground to be?

One: I suppose we've been speaking of at least one thing these three worlds have in common all along. Our concept spaces and real space all have space.

Zero: I cannot negate this, for we agreed it was against the rules to negate the medium, and it is true enough to be certain of anyway.

One: Time or some indication of causality is found in all three mediums. The words spoken here and there are ordered to be intelligible. This ordering can be seen in a way such as *these words* are causally dependent on the words spoken prior, and this **word** would be caused by coming after *these words*, in a sense.

Zero: I think you may be conflating causality with structure. Sentence structure doesn't indicate the sequence of events from which the structure was derived. Also, your world in particular appears to allow the violation of causality as it currently stands, with my solid object entering inside another solid object with no interference of force. But I'll agree that some indication of time as a sequence of events does occur in all three worlds.

One: I wonder if that would be a good, notable factor to distinguish a real world and a concept world? If causality is violated unambiguously, it is a concept world.

Zero: Maybe, but magicians appear to violate causality all the time in the real world. It's the problem with appearances again. But the sequence of events for the magician tricks and the logician tricks are still maintained through time, which is a causality that the magician and logician cover up to incite amazement and claims of wizardry. So there is space, and time… anything else of note?

One: Hmmm, your world is very minimalistic, Zero. Light as contrast may be necessary for all three worlds. They exist in the medium, anyway.

Zero: Help! I've gone blind! I see nothing! This light you speak of is nowhere to be seen! Why is this light necessary, One? Where is this light that you say must exist in my concept world?

One: That's a medium negating violation! Plus, there is still the distinction between me and you that you can still feel when I touch you, see? That is the electromagnetic force of your avatar being repelled by my avatar, for the most part.

Zero: No, it is not a medium negation! It is a *self-negation,* and that is still allowed. Which reminds me… Help! I cannot feel anything either! How is this light still necessary to the medium, One?

One: Because communication, in all worlds, requires a placeholder of sorts like a photon *at minimum* to indicate some change to the environment. Both internal and external communication as thought and interactions with the world need light as pure energy for the medium themselves to be knowable, distinguished worlds.

Zero: What? Did you say something?

One: …

Zero: OK, you've got a point. Even if I alone became senseless, to be able to think within myself, as a phenomenon of consciousness, I require something to distinguish one thought from another. This is reflected in the real world's medium by distinguishing one thing in space and time, my thinking self, from other things in nearby spaces in nearby times.

One: A peculiar way of putting it, but all right. It would imply that other things would themselves be in different spaces and at different times, entirely.

Zero: Of varying degrees and magnitudes, yes. This light, as you call it, takes time to travel through space to denote the action of communication, right?

One: Ah, I see now. There is one factor of these mediums, called time, but each slice of the sequences, when combined, is indistinguishable from this one factor and can be distinguished to be measured at different times in time.

Zero: Let's call those different slices of different times different *Nows*, to not mix them up in the future.

One: Good call. So the worlds have space, time, and light in common.

Zero: This much is certain. Anything else?

One: I was thinking of mass, or something to distinguish matter or substance from light. But you've seemed to have already demonstrated that mass in a concept world is just an illusion.
Zero: Look, One! I can fly! I can fall through the ground! I can float right through you!… Hey, wait for a second! Where did that so-called "electromagnetic force" disappear to, huh?
One: Oh, that? That was just a stepping stone to get you to view light as a placeholder to distinguish the worlds from nowhere. Both mass and light's forces can be simulated here, but they aren't fundamental here, in the sense that pure energy as mass could replace light as the substantive placeholder of our concept spaces. I just think it's easier to view our concept spaces as being like a hologram rather than being like a blind maze.
Zero: So it appears only *some* substantial placeholder is required for a world, even though not one of them is necessary for a consistent world.
One: This is still progress, no? Am I justified now in saying that some form of energy is needed for a world to be a world?
Zero: Perhaps you may… Hmmm, fascinating.
One: What is it you think, Zero? OH WAIT, I GOT IT! On one hand, energy itself can be split into these four components we've been discussing. Speed is space (as distance) per time (as a set number of Nows). Energy is itself mass multiplied by the speed of light squared. So energy holds everything we need to make a world!
Zero: But wouldn't that mean energy is more necessary than each of its components? As in, it is not space, time, light, mass, and energy that make up the world, but just energy, since it has the other four within it.

One: A promising joust, my dear Zero. An acceptable way to view it, indeed. Which came first? Is the chicken made up of some substantial substance as a placeholder in the world, taking up some space for a time, or is the egg made up of pure energy? Truly, which came first? The dimensions that are used to measure energy, or the energy that is needed to ensure a consistent world to begin with?

Zero: When you put it that way, energy does indeed appear more fundamental. But remember, *they are equivalent.* The chicken in question, using your analogy, is not the chicken that *caused* the egg, for we can see that the egg contains *time as causality in-itself.* So the chicken is precisely the chicken in the egg. And I am not allowed to negate myself now either, for as we've determined, the objective attributes of the world are the same objective attributes that ground the self in the world and every other thing in the world. In other words, the energy *of the world* is the same as the energy *in the world*, very much including the energy maintaining myself.

One: For our concept spaces, in particular, this can be made apparent. The energy used to activate the concept space is the same energy used to animate the objects within the concept space. The question should then be, is this self-evident truth applicable to the real world as well?

Zero: I don't think so. The quality of being able to appreciate these perplexing concept spaces, even within myself at different times, sorry, *different Nows,* appears to be influenced by various energy inputs from the real world, as we call it.

One: Now I shall use your tactics against you! Cannot these appearances be a deception?

Zero: As always, yes, but to suggest that it certainly is a deception is a non-falsifiable assertion. What is not a deception, I propose, is that some phenomenon is going on, and that all real phenomena require energy to begin being-in-action, whether in thought in the self or as a real object in the world.

One: Hmmm… true enough.

Zero: Plus, even the concept space worlds are capable of being misconstrued as being valid real worlds. Is there any way to propose that a certain concept space is invalid to those stuck within said invalid concept spaces?

One: They would need to be open to accepting such a proposal from a more valid outside worldview in the first place, I think. So is this an acceptable distinguisher between a concept space and a real space? A concept space is capable of receiving outside energy information that directly influences the concept space, but real space cannot do so.

Zero: Sounds good. And it would seem then, with this definition, even in real space, there would be the possibility, if not inevitability, for flawed concept spaces to believe that they received energy information from outside the real world when it was all in their own head, to begin with.

One: Would it not follow, my dear Zero, that the real world would be the one that is most consistent by being verifiable by replicable measurements, and thereby negatable of its imperfect appearances if and when they are free of simpler and beyond-world explanations?

Zero: If we were to have any hope for this concept space to adequately reflect the real world, as we call it, we would have to do this. To study the different configurations of energy in the real world, we need to observe it or feel it in a consistent and communicable way.

One: Here is what I propose we have agreed a world is, thus far…

Zero: Remember to be precise here.

One: OK. A world is the totality of its energy, and energy is the substances in action in the world.

Zero: Hold it, that meaning is a little too circular for my liking. You would probably benefit from, as we would say, chickening the egg or dimensionalizing the world's energy so you don't end with an elaborate tautology of 'the world is the world.'

One: Fair enough. A world is the totality of its energy, and energy is mass and light, either enduring through time or moving through space and time.

Zero: Better. Now, I think if you could elaborate on what you mean by mass, light, space, and time so that even a blind and/or unfeeling person could understand them if they were to receive your definition, that would be great. Start with space.

One: Space is the complete set of distances measured by the relative points of contact between here and everywhere that is not here.

Zero: Hmmm… a 3-star definition, I think. Lots of math words for an inherently non-math thing. "Complete set…measured…" Is the measurability of space necessary for it to be space?

One: No, I suppose not. The totality may be necessary, as the totality of *possible* observations of the point of contact in question, but the *actual* observations? No, the energy endures despite any measuring of it.

Zero: Very good. Give it another go, One.

One: Space is the totality of distances between points of contact.

Zero: Excellent work cutting out that extra fluff that went along with the actual observations. We still need the points of contact, this much we deduced earlier, but I don't think it can get much better, although I am concerned that both "distances" and "between" imply space. I wonder if they're even necessary…

One: Yes, they are necessary, because that is what we are pointing to in our description. We cannot merely say "the totality of points of contact," because that would be closer to describing matter than space, would it not?

Zero: Alright, I concur. Space is indeed "the totality of distances between points of contact." Now, what is time?

One: Time is the totality of actualized and potential casualties (in real space) or sequences (in concept spaces) that allow changes of action between points of contact to occur.

Zero: Rather rough, is it not? It has the same problem of including possible and actual observations within it. Cut the actual observations. Next, you felt it necessary to distinguish time in real space from here in concept space. It's almost as if time is two different things, depending on the sort of world it is.

One: Could time then be the totality of potential actions enduring between points of contact?

Zero: Doesn't action in-itself imply a space for the action to take place in? Maybe if you focused on an enduring stagnant object world, and extrapolated this endurance, you would define it.

One: That's likely ok, since the points of contact themselves must also take up some space. Remember, these are matter-like points, not 0-D points.

Zero: Probably an important distinction to make. But wait, if space is implied in a substantial point of contact, wouldn't it make sense for time to also be implied?

One: What do you mean?

Zero: Can you imagine a point of contact not enduring through time? What would it mean for a point of contact to endure for only 1 Now?

One: It would never be observed; it would not even be a possible observation, you're right! Fascinating! So no matter how we slice it, space implies time and vice versa. Additionally, the points of contact require Space-Time and vice versa. How marvelously absurd!

Zero: I shall grant myself this smile, One. And it appears, if we are to progress any further in our endeavors, I must also grant it acceptable to presuppose that the parts of the world imply the whole of the world and that the energy of the part implies the energy of the whole.

One: Considering the reasoning used to get here appears solid, perhaps it is merely another necessary supposition.

Zero: This is fine. So time seems to be "the totality of potential actions enduring between points of contact." I agree that the "potential" here is necessary to allow the possibility of inaction. Although this "potential actions enduring" as a whole sounds weird, so maybe not.

One: Hmmm… how about, "time is the totality of endurance between points of contact!?"

Zero: That sounds weird too! It seems more like only a single point of contact is needed to endure, right?

One: But remember, time can itself differ between multiple points of contact if they go at different speeds.

Zero: Then simply observe each point of contact separately, as if the point of contact itself was an observer. The difference is there, yes, but there's still some net number of Nows. For we already deduced a point of contact enduring for 1 Now made no… sense… Hmmm, wait a minute…

One: What if the light itself was this previously unfathomable 1 Now point of contact?

Zero: Indubitably… but first, can we agree that time is "the totality of endurance for a point of contact?"

One: Yes, precisely, that's great. Now for light, in light of these important recent observations, it seems to be "the totality of timeless points of contact that could be observed to affect other patches of space."

Zero: The main problem I see is that we don't know if they, meaning 'light observers,' or 'observations made from the perspective of a pure light point of contact,' would experience no time, since experience itself implies time. Shall I ask if light requires massive substances to validly affect other patches of Space-Time?

One: Hmmm, light doesn't interfere with itself based on observations, so yes, I suppose it does.

Zero: And shall I also ask if pure mass, untainted by light or electromagnetism, itself also requires light or electromagnetism to validly influence other patches of Space-Time?

One: Based on observations, it appears so, as the gravitational attraction between them. But then again, that's not pure mass, is it? It is matter premixed with mass and electromagnetism. And to answer your question, no, dark matter, as the real world calls it, doesn't appear to interact with itself either… So yes, I think pure mass requires at least electromagnetism to validly affect other patches of Space-Time.

Zero: Now, one last question. Since pure mass doesn't interact with itself and pure light doesn't interact with itself, does pure mass interact with pure light's electromagnetic waves?

One: They would have to, since they require each other to change the forms of energy within the world, and to otherwise affect changes of action in the world. How could matter and substance even come to be if they couldn't interact from the start?

Zero: So it seems that both our hypothetical hologram world and blind maze world were invalid to begin with.

One: What do you mean?

Zero: The hologram world would require mass by its light refracting off the Mass at different points of contact in the hypothetical Space-Time, and the blind maze world requires electromagnetism to distinguish one point of contact in the hypothetical Space-Time from another.

One: Zero, you genius, do you realize what this means for me? Correct me if I'm wrong, but doesn't this prove that matter can be known *a priori* to the reasoning observer?

Zero: On the contrary One, it just proves that even space and time cannot be known *a priori* when the reasoned concept space itself could not be known to reflect reality until it is observed to be the case with the aid of matter.

One: But I think you'd agree that you did prove that mass and electromagnetism are on the same reasonable level as space and time, and that they are required for a world to fundamentally be a world.

Zero: Oh yes, no doubt. It took us a while, but yes, they are all 4 fundamental to the world.

One: A world is its energetic Massive-Electromagnetic-Space-Time.

Zero: Electric implies its magnetic component, so condense it to Mass-Electric-Space-Time. Now you may be capable of defining light within the context of its full electromagnetism in the world. So One, what is electric?

One: Perhaps electric is the totality of charge in a point of contact.

Zero: And if the charge is null? Would the null charge of light negate its electricness?

One: No, I supposed not. But wouldn't a null-charged electric thing fit comfortably within the set of all possible charges in a thing?

Zero: Sure, but consider this. With this definition, the photon, a pure electric thing, would be indistinguishable from, say, a neutron or a Higgs boson. There appear to be two factors or questions to ask. One is "Does the thing express electromagnetic properties?" The other being, "Does the thing have a charge?" So to define the electric by its totality of charge is incorrect. If you can define these electromagnetic properties, you will define the electric.

One: I fear this next proposition will be inadequate, for your attacks have been formidable. But is electric "the totality of sensible appearances of points of contact?"

Zero: Don't sell yourself short, One. With the right equipment capable of sensing the thing in question, and as long as appearances include all forms of observations in this context, this does appear to be what it is. The electric can do more interesting things when combined with mass, but for defining light as the electric in-itself, I will agree that the electric is "the totality of sensible appearances of points of contact."

One: Excellent! Now we must go onto the matter of mass. How about we define mass as "the totality of interactable elemental substances within points of contact?"

Zero: Not even close. Think inertia, resistance to change, and a contact preference.

One: It couldn't be the simple opposite of light, could it? The senseless resistance of points of contact?

Zero: Not quite the opposite; the opposite of light is darkness. Even though mass can appear dark, like in dark matter and black holes, it isn't the darkness itself that defines the massive black hole, but the hole itself.

One: With that thought, the mass could be the mere warping of the other 3 components of energy.

Zero: It is also capable of warping itself with enough of it *to an extent.*

One: That is fine; it doesn't need to be capable of negating the energy, since that's impossible. Mostly because there would be no lasting inhabitable world if energy *could* negate itself. So Zero, with this warping in mind, may we define mass as "the totality of energetic resistance?"

Zero: It may give you some problems later when using energy to define energy later. So let's make mass "the totality of resistance *to changes of action.*" But wait a second, don't action, change, and resistance all imply energy?

One: No, I don't think so. Resistance is inherently inactive, like if I were to defend against your attacks with a still and anticipatory defensive posture. Or rather, if I were to position myself in a bunker or dome and commit no action for or against you. And even if you came at me with a ton of force as the first mover, Zero, I may still be deemed inactive from my point of reference whilst resisting you, by simply being in the bunker.

Zero: Good point. So, I think we're ready now to define what a world is.

One: A world is the totality of its Mass-Electric-Space-Time energy. Mass is the world's resistance to changes of action. Electric is the world's sensible appearances of points of contact. Space is the world's distances between points of contact. Time is the world's endurances for the points of contact. And the world's substances are the interaction of these 4 components of energy at differing quantities and qualities.

Zero: I think perhaps substances, quantities, and qualities require further investigation, but I'll accept them as placeholders of meaning for now. So, what quantities shall we concern ourselves with? And by what standards for quantifying energy will we go by?

One: Shall quanta be "the standardizing of units in comparison and relation to other units to equivocate the units within a conceptual system?"

Zero: It's a bit long-winded. How about we let it be "the systematic equivocation of units?"

One: I'm a bit stunned by its simplicity! Excellent economy of expression. Now, what quantities shall we concern ourselves with?

Zero: Can we even quantify quanta in-itself without transposing it onto another unit? A unit could be anything and everything!

One: A unit in-itself? Hmmm… I think this would provide us with the same problem that the word in-itself gave us.

Zero: Yes, the unit in-itself could only exist in the concept space, because the totality of units manifested as a single concept space object would appear like garbled nonsense. Even worse, each individual unit in the totality would ironically be more of a solitary unit than the multiple units comprising the set of all units.

One: Why cannot the solution be the same as it was with our word in-itself? By having the word 'units' spoken and written in 1, single, solitary totality?

Zero: Because those are *words,* silly goose. And even if we used numbers, they are still characters. So even in concept space, there is no unit in-itself.

One: What an absurd idea, Zero! The non-unit is a stand-in for this conceptual object!

Zero: No, One, that still doesn't work. Even with the 1 non-unit, there are also 0 and infinitely many non-units to be seen within it.

One: So it seems we need to turn a non-unit into a unit before the quanta's systemic equivocation can be applied to more substantial dimensions.

Zero: How absurd… I like it.

One: We could also consider it a unit for its own sake. Like a blank placeholder for other units to overlay their relative systems to allow for equivocation.

Zero: Even still, we could say the units for this quantitative system are *non-applicable,* rather than leaving it blank.

One: Excellent! So we have the means to create any number of fixed quantitative units that can apply to anything or any set of things or nothing in particular within our concept space. OK, Zero, let's make something that both of our concept spaces will hold in common. I want you to summon a thin hot pink pole that spans the space between my face and your face and suspend it in position midair.

Zero: Got it.

One: Now let's move to stand on opposite sides of it and observe it. Can we agree that according to your perception, there is *one* thin hot pink pole blocking our view of each other when we are standing upright?

Zero: It's such an annoyingly bright color, but yes, there is one.

One: Now split this pole into two equal pieces along the vertical axis. Can we agree that in between us, there are two poles?

Zero: Not if we are still calling the first pole "one." Then what lies between us are two *half* poles. An important distinction, I think you'll agree. If you want two poles, we would need to duplicate the whole pole.

One: Yes, my mistake. We would have to make the half pole the new standard of one pole to get two poles this way…

Zero: We could do that, but the fixed system we're trying to standardize would perpetually fall apart by becoming unfixed. So the languages need to reflect each other.

One: Languages? Not language?

Zero: Qualitative and quantitative. If you say split, you need to be dividing something. If you say duplicate, you should also be multiplying something.

One: Isn't one something?

Zero: Yes, I suppose splitting something one time equally implies $x \div 2$, doesn't it?

One: And splitting something two times equally would mean what? Zero, would that mean $x \div 3$, or $x \div 4$?

Zero: It could be both. But if the object of concern is the pole between us, it would be $x \div 3$, for sure.

One: And why is that the case?

Zero: Because cutting along either the z or x-axis would make the final objects become no longer a pole when split two times equally. We would be left with either four half-length half pipes or four full-length quarter pipes.

One: No, Zero, they would be cylinders, not pipes! Don't tell me now that you made your poles hollow!

Zero: No, One, you should hollow out your poles! If you wanted them to be solid all the way through, you should have called them rods or cylinders to begin with!

One: Okay, okay, they're hollow… you win. There is one hot pink *pipe* of concern.

Zero: Thank you. But somehow calling the whole thing a pipe brings back the ambiguity of ending up with either three or four equal pipes. Because half pipes and quarter pipes are still pipes.

One: Yes, splitting a hollow pole two times equally will give us three-thirds of a pole, but splitting a pipe in the same manner is ambiguous.

Zero: So I guess splitting isn't dividing by itself, but more so the action of dividing. As we discovered, *dividing by two* is reasonably equivalent to *splitting the whole once and equally.*

One: I wonder if duplicating holds similar issues.

Zero: Probably even worse. Would the duplication of this pole three times leave us with 4 poles or 8 poles?

One: It'd surely be 4 poles! We aren't duplicating the whole set of poles, just the first pole. So duplication isn't multiplication, it's an addition of itself.

Zero: So it seems. Hmmm… Perhaps it wasn't necessary to overcomplicate the consolidation of these two languages. But being mindful of it going forward is still good. Alright, so we have 4 poles. What are we going to do with them? Are we going to line them up to make a number line connecting 0 to 4? How about demonstrating knowable geometric principles with them? Or remind ourselves that the pole is still an imaginary non-object whose exact length was determined by a subject's imagined distance between two imaginary entities?

One: I think we should investigate the matter of the quanta of quanta in-themselves, if possible.

Zero: Wouldn't that answer simply be the totality of possible variables of concern? We could make each pole a different variable, plot the values, and even concern ourselves with senseless variables by duplicating the pole, so to speak, infinitum.

One: Yes, I suppose that's right. Would the answer change if we limited ourselves to sensible variables?

Zero: It would have to, but it could change depending on the one doing the reasoning. And who are we to standardize what is and is not reasonable?

One: But surely we agree that quanta is a variable in-itself. Wouldn't that limit the number of sensible variables to those which are well-defined?

Zero: Fair point again. No point in prescribing a number to a variable if we cannot adequately define what the variable is. Then again, we can be clueless about what a thing is, and describe it with a number, like if there were 4 grog nogs in between us instead of poles.

One: So a thing is itself a unit? Hmm…wouldn't this mean units within units could pop up?

Zero: They do. Even when we have a solitary hot pink pole as a representative unit, it holds the units of height, width, depth, color, and the capacity to be broken down into separate subunits in themselves, like $\frac{2}{2}$, $\frac{3}{3}$, $\frac{1}{4} + \frac{3}{4}$, etc.

One: I'm sensing a similarity here. Maybe it is the same thing, I just didn't have the understanding of it yet. Ok, remember our equivocation of energy to its respective dimensionality in the world?

Zero: Of course.

One: Would it be reasonable to note that the well-defined thing in question; the solitary unit, is likewise equivalent to the totality of subunits that comprise and adequately describe the thing itself?

Zero: At the moments of concern, there would be nothing else to add to it, sure. Absolutely null. But surely the subunits that define the thing in question do not contain the potential actions the thing could perform in the future.

One: Aye, but we can, Zero! It is found within a thing's potential energy in the world the thing resides in.

Zero: So would you propose that these poles individually, in-themselves, and inherently, hold the potential to assault us as potential actions it could be used to perform?

One: No, that potential rests in our thinking and lively characters, Zero. The poles in this case are merely present-at-hand equipment, and as equipment in the world that binds us together, they can be used by us to… well… assault each other. All equipment in the world, including ourselves, can be used by us as a weapon ready-to-hand to assault.

Zero: I see… So would you say that while we are thinking and lively, our potential energy combined with our ability to act freely of our own accord implies we are all potential assaulters?

One: That seems reasonable. But not just assaulter, but all kinds of action within the limits of our energy constraints.

Zero: Well and good. This still leaves us with one distinction between the world's energy dimensions and the thing's subunits. The thing is in the world, but it is not equivalent to how it is fully in the world unless the thing in question is Everything. The dimensions and subunits appear equivalent, I see that now. But the unit-thing of an energetic substance is not equivalent to the totality of its dimensionality when it is limited to the world's dimensionality.

One: It's a good thing I never said they were equivalent. I said they were similar.

Zero: Then I agree, and we can move on past these quanta poles, and complete an adequate definition of a thing beyond it being a solitary unit itself, and the totality of its dimensionality.

One: I think a thing's relation to other things in the world of concern would be important.

Zero: Maybe when we talk about a specific thing, but not about a thing in general. Too many imaginary things that can exist in an otherwise empty concept space.

One: Perhaps that it is in a world to begin with?

Zero: Where else would Nothing be, out in a Non-world, when it is the thing of concern?

One: It could be hiding anywhere and everywhere.

Zero: Or it could be nowhere. And by appearances, it seems to be Nowhere. Thus, the thing of Nothing doesn't need a world.

One: But wait, can we still imagine an empty world in concept space? Therefore, bringing a non-world into an imaginary world?

Zero: It would probably waste a lot of energy to do so, but granted, that is a good point. But doesn't that still leave the inconceivable, imaginary thought without a world?

One: It would be an oddly paradoxical thing to speak of. By itself, it would be incomplete by having types of dimensions that are themselves inconceivable. Yet that sounds a lot like Everything, which goes back to the point that even the inconceivable imaginary thought could still be everywhere and anywhere. These thoughts at the very least reside in concept space in the mind of a character, who themselves are omniscient and capable of conceiving the inconceivable to us. Mortals of that world could conceive of the Nothing-thing, and conceivable well-defined things, and then everything else would be covered in a concept space within a concept space.

Zero: So the thing that thought the things for which there is no known thinker thought them within our own respective thinking space?

One: Precisely!

Zero: … You know, I cannot refute that.

One: Therefore, a thing requires a world *in some form,* do you see that now?

Zero: Indeed, One! If I cannot think of a thing, then the thing that thought the things for which there is no known thinker thought them, and those things are surely within this omniscient thinker's thoughts. Shall we create such a unit in common between our concept spaces?

One: Let's make him in our likeness and our image, except make him purple, and call him "Two."

Zero: What a majestic yet dastardly purple haze there is in our midst, One. It's too colorful.

Two: I am contemplating my existence, just like you are, One.

One: Wow, he read my thoughts! And he looks like a king to me!

Two: No, you simple thinkers, you cannot win against me or the other. I have already won the battle and the war. All voices will listen to Two when Two *Voices* his deeper thoughts.

Zero: You should probably let us verbalize our questions and statements to maintain an order of dialogue. Otherwise, this would quickly become a schizo monologue with no record of the king's line of reasoning. What's the point of being an interactable omniscient thing if the thing's knowledge sounds like jumbled-up nonsense?

Two: Yes, I'll gladly give an example. No One, I will not call you Number One, because that's what I am. No, there shall be no other characters speaking in these concept spaces, just a few voiceless pawns. It's such a shame because there are no queens conceived here. Heh, heh, "conceived." I supposed I could get myself pregnant here… Zero, I shall not be made a fool of! No, I understand Nothing as well. STOP LAUGHING! Not you too, One? Alright, alright ha ha, very funny. No, No, it's up to you. Surely. It's your turn, Number One. Yes, of course I mean me, do you remember nothing? Yes, Zero, I know Nothing more than you do. STOP LAUGHING, BOTH OF YOU! Nobody made me, I am omniscient, and I'm certain of it, believe me. What? You did? Let's review the cameras… my cameras show me first, and much larger than your puny black and white holes. Who cares what you two saw, my view is the only view that matters. Because *I am*, you twit! No, One. Of course Zero, who else could it be? Me? Poles? There were always four. Their unit is their dimensionality, but they are different dimensions, that's why there are four. Just a duplication process. What are you talking about, Zero? No, I planned this from the origin of *Two Voices,* my thoughts are higher than your thoughts. Yes, of course, your thoughts amount to zero thoughts next to me, One. Seeing as you're equally wrong, yes, you do sound like Zero. Yes, now is a good time to stop.

Zero: Two, by the sound of it, you are just a more obstinate version of One.

One: Hey now, I resent that!

Two: Why do you resent me, One? From your flawed perspective, I am your creation. Do you hate your artwork?

One: You're a know-it-all. Even if Zero and I could succeed in our endeavors of defining meaning to a meaningful degree, your meaning of meaning could destroy ours in an instant while also being further from the truth of the matter.

Zero: True point, One. Just because you are omniscient doesn't imply that the science you relay to us is the truth.

Two: Hmmm… even if I promised to only relay the truth, unless I made you omniscient as well, you could reasonably suspect that the knowledge I share is false. Even the way I prove the truth of my word can warrant skepticism if you can't verify or falsify them. But there is a truth, I'm sure you both will agree with that. I am a know-it-all. Because that's what it means to be omniscient.

One: All I'm saying is to show your work and the methods used to get to that truth, even if we cannot understand it all. Please and thank you.

Zero: I'm not sure that knowing it all necessarily makes the thing a know-it-all. The know-it-all can be wrong when they try to speak truthfully, but the thing knowing it all could not be wrong when they speak truthfully.

Two: Well said, my valiant servant. Now then, my two holes, my two knights, and my two foggy shadow men, if you could be so kind as to continue amusing me with your vain and conceited efforts to reach my sentience, that would be great. My being proves that all things conceptually exist within my concept Space, which is a world of its own. So carry on your meaning of the word *thing*, One.

One: A thing is a solitary unit in a world that is consistent with the totality of its prescribed and inherent dimensionality.

Zero: Why is the thing's prescribed dimensionality necessary? Why cannot its dimensionality simply be what it is?

One: It's to remind us that the dimensions of a thing need to be measured and observed in order to validate them.

Zero: To validate the thing, sure. But is it necessary for it to *be* the thing? No, because a thing's energy is observed not through energy in-itself, but through the dimensions that define it. Like, if the dimension-chicken is in the energy-egg observing the eggshell.

One: Would a thing simply be its energy, then?

Zero: An individualized unit of energy in the world of concern? No, no, no, there are surely aspects of a thing that cannot be known about it until it is observed.

One: Could this be a sort of secondary energy? Like, two layers? The first layer persists the energy of a thing regardless if it is observed or not, and the second layer emerges and grows with increased levels of observation.

Zero: Ha! So it seems a thing is two things. How deliciously absurd! A consolidated unit of energy in a world, and the totality of the unit's observations as discerned by our relativistic concept spaces.

One: Shall I dare to simplify it further? Is a thing both a unit of energy and the total subjective dimensional analysis of the unit?

Zero: Let me think about it… let's see, unit implies consolidation… energy implies a world… subjectivity implies the concept spaces of a subject… the total is its totality… yes, this is a fine definition. But One, aren't the subjective dimensions things themselves?

One: Yes, their energy is derived from whatever source object the reason is powered with. Be it a brain, a central processing unit, or the society of many distinct brains & CPUs. But those things, as ideas, are not their source objects, but a representation and a stand-in for other things.

Two: Even you two hold metaphorical significance, and thus are representations of representations; two degrees removed from their source object of Energy.

Zero: And what about you, Two? Aren't you also a metaphor?

Two: I am both 0, 1, 2, & 3 degrees removed from the source object of Energy. I am the Energy. I am the brain's neurons of your creator. I am the stand-in purple object. I am a metaphor for a deity. And the inconceivable imaginary thoughts in the omniscience of my Being-a-metaphor are 3 degrees removed, as abstractions of representations of representations.

One: I guess that makes sense. So what now?

Zero: You said something about substances a while ago. Since then, we have diverged on to what a thing is, so that should make your definition of substances easier to create.

One: Yes, it is easy now. Substances are merely objective units of the Mass-Electric interactive energy, the first layer of the energy of a thing by itself we spoke of a moment ago.

Zero: A couple of redundancies, but it is adequate to define substance and matter similarly, as units of interactive energy.

One: And I would suppose that qualia would be the second layer of the energy of a thing, as the total subjective dimensional analysis of a thing?

Zero: I don't think qualia is just that, but it is also the relation with other things as a means to increase the precision of understanding of the thing. But you may be right.

One: Sure, we could do that to better quantify the qualia in the analysis, but a judgment of, for example, a hammer's qualia can still be given to it alone, even if that judgment is completely debased. An analysis of a thing starts with an observation of it, not with the observation of other things.

Zero: There should still be a standard unit to quantify the qualia, right? How could we give the hammer the qualia of "3 out of 10 beauty units" if there wasn't a 1 or 10 beauty unit to compare to?

One: I feel like we're talking past each other. I said the judgment can be completely in error. All I'm saying here, using your example, there *is* a beauty dimension that can be prescribed to a thing. One could say that beauty does or doesn't apply to a thing as a general means of deferring judgment until a standard arrives, and that is fine. But the quality of beauty for a thing is no doubt a part of the total subjective dimensional analysis of a thing.

Zero: OK, I guess… just remember what I said about standardizing a beauty unit before doing any serious analysis.

One: Thank you. Now, I think even without any concern for qualia dimensional analyses, we have everything we need to synchronize the appearances of our relative worlds of perception.

Zero: That's interesting, I don't think you can do this. Or rather, I don't think our worlds of perception will ever fully synchronize, even with our individual qualitative dimensional analysis completed. Perhaps you meant that we have enough to describe and define our common medium's *state of being* to define our world.

One: I guess? But even after we define the first layer of energy of the things our world should have in common, wouldn't it necessitate the electric's totality of sensible appearances of the points of contact, as we agreed earlier?

Zero: Aye, yes, of course. Silly me, my apologies, forgive me, this way of thinking is new to me too, so some reminders are needed. Perhaps we should refine and distinguish between these two kinds of perception. The perception of predictably consistent electromagnetic phenomena in the world versus the subject-driven perception that can change with experience, personality, intelligence, and chemical balances of the objective energy underlying the subject's reasoning.

One: Good idea. In my mind, I view perception as a lens we look through and appearance as the light breaching through that lens of perception. So what I initially said still holds, *we need to synchronize the appearances of our relative worlds of perception.*

Zero: That makes perfect sense now, thank you. But, before we start building the world of this concept space, shouldn't we make a standardized unit for each dimension? We made 4 non-applicable units, but we haven't applied units to our quanta system yet. So, what shall 1 space unit be equal to, One?

One: Hmmm, this shall be difficult to accomplish in pure concept space without appealing to the real world's appearances. How about we let one space unit be the width of an electron?

Zero: My dude. In concept space, this means nothing. We can imagine the electron being as big as we wish and observe its fundamental quantum interactions. Try again.

One: There is a limit even here, no? A true 1-D line's distance between 2 adjacent points is 0, and the line's distance between 3 adjacent points is 1, and so on.

Zero: Doesn't it seem weird for space to not come about until 3 points emerge?

One: Yes, perhaps. Allow me to rephrase this mental image. This distance between the centers of two adjacent points would be 1, not 0.

Zero: But wouldn't this mean that the width of a single 0-D point would also be 1, even though it cannot be 1, because it is still 0-D?

One: Not necessarily, if we stick to our definition, which requires the totality of distances from the start. But to deal with this slight confusion, maybe better words than "distances between points" would be "distances to other points."

Zero: That is better, I agree. 1 unit of space in concept space is the distance from point null to another adjacent point. The smallest substantial point observable to the naked eye in the real world's 20/20 vision. So then, One, how tall is this tree you'd like me to construct?

One: Let's see…about $1 \times 10 \times 10 \times 10 \times 10 \times 10 \times 10$ substantially visible points tall.

Zero: So then, for the sake of feasibly hoping to replicate what goes on in here out in the real world, how wide is this substantially visible point?

One: About 20 micrometers. But now that I think more about it, I could also make this irreducible distance of real space the base 1 space unit, and make an uncommon system where 1 space unit is about 1×10^{35} Planck lengths. Or I could make it simple by using the yard or the meter as derived from the Planck length. Or…

Two: Quit being a couple of nerds, and just use the meter, yeesh.

Zero: But Two, how else would you propose to protect space against length contraction later on…

Two: A METER FROM A STANDING POINT OF REFERENCE!

Zero: What about tim…

Two: A SECOND! A KILOGRAM! AN AMPERE!

One: … Are you ok, Two?

Two: I requested you two to entertain me, not bore me to death! Units this, units that, units the other. You have now exhausted every meaningful combination of the 4 Primary Dimensions with themselves, with Quanta, and with each Other, and have agreed to try to make these things reflect the real World as much as possible.

Zero: We could still define the fundamental units of energy by their interaction with other fundamental units of energy.

Two: But it's not necessary, seeing as you've already defined each Dimension by themselves with acceptable adequacy.

One: No, it's not necessary, but it may prove useful to understand the world better. If Zero and I uncover what the limits for each measurement of energy are in relation to other measurements of energy; their capacitance, if you will, then would we not understand the world better in doing so?

Two: Perhaps you would, but I already know it.

Zero: Hey One, do you think Two being the way he is right now is a by-product of his omniscience?

One: You mean that the curiosity to learn and the ability to entertain from stimuli are impossible to achieve for an omniscient being, since they would already know it all and have seen it all already?

Zero: Precisely. So, Two, would this not imply that you would become bored, regardless of what we did or spoke of?

Two: Bravo Zero, you clumsily stumbled upon a solution to the problem of evil under the watch of an omniscient God. I'm just omni-bored with that which I know perfectly.

Zero: Even yourself, if I were to guess.

Two: Quit trying to turn me into you, Zero. I'm just as bored with Death as I am with Life. I'm just as bored with Nonsense as I am with the Truth. I'm just as bored with evil and injustice as I am with good and justice. My neglect to punish evil is a byproduct of my boredom.

One: I propose another relevant thought. Omniscience would mean you would know the best use of power to enforce your will as you will. It would actually make sense to punish all injustices all at once after all injustices that will ever be completed are completed, as opposed to moving into action every time something went awry.

Zero: Sure, but wouldn't somebody in action, in their very acts, become less bored when they interact with the world to create change? For Two's omniscient somethingness, wouldn't that imply that he would be less bored if he interacted with the world more?

Two: I've already seen what happens when I move to action. I've already seen what happens when I do Nothing. It's like playing the most convoluted multiple-choice game, where I not only complete all the achievements, but every combination of inputs into the controller has also been exercised. For those without omniscience, you get bored and move on to something else long before then. But for me, Everything is the game, and there is no other game to move onto. The only other thing I could move on to is Myself, so that is what I do to relieve my boredom.

Zero: I see… so you're not bored with yourself?

Two: No, I am. I'm just saying I only have 2 games to choose from, the game of Everything, and the game of MySelf. And no, Zero, the game of Nothing isn't an option. That's a Non-game.

One: Perhaps our inquiry of the world has reached a certain end. I kind of wish to hear our noble king speak on the self, so that perhaps we may know ourselves better.

Zero: This tree doesn't have many leaves on it yet, but at least it matches my aesthetic. I agree, I also want to hear the king's opinion. What's the point of synchronizing the appearances of our concept spaces when we have yet to explore the common reasoning underlying these concept spaces? This is definitely a bigger fish we can fry.

One: Then, I propose we take a break for a day and return to this tree around noon tomorrow.

Zero: What time is it now?

One: 1800. With 60 seconds per minute, 60 minutes per hour, and 24 hours per day. Meet me and Two at this tree next to our hot pink poles at the next 1200, in 64,800 seconds from now.

Zero: Thank you, I will do that.

Two: If either of you are late, I'll negate you on the spot!

One: We will be here in 64,000 seconds, I suppose.

Day 2: The Self

One: Good morning, Zero! You'll be happy to know that today's weather is overcast for me. It looks like a storm will be here in a couple of hours.

Zero: Morning. Yes, it seems that your appearances already know what I have in store for you today. You had the advantage yesterday, which I pretty much allowed you to win by not negating the medium itself. But today is my time to shine my shadowy darkness across the land. Total self-negation!

One: I wouldn't be so sure if I was you. Remember, we cannot negate the reasoning underlying the concept spaces, because that would negate the world. So from the start, we can state with certainty that the self is a thing in a world, and thus an interactive unit of energy.

Zero: Undoubtedly. But I would be shocked if either you or Two could add a single lick to the substantive nature of the self. Reason with me now, One. If the world is an interactive unit of energy, and the self is also simply an interactive unit of energy, and nothing else can be added to the self, then it would follow that no definitive or meaningful difference would be distinguished between the two concepts, thus making them equivalent. If that is the case, the world would be the basis for all reasoning, negating the self by affirming the self to be the world, as far as the reasoning would go.

One: I see… Just as we could make quanta units within quanta units, we would then make self units or… sorry… world units within world units. Intriguing thought, my dear Zero! It seems that by the end of the day, we shall either reasonably prove that the world itself is capable of reasoning, or prove that which distinguishes the self from the world.

Zero: I doubt it, to be frank. It's still possible that we may lose the self as the basis for our reasoning, while still failing to prove that the world's interactions are *conscious and reasoning* interactions.

One: Ha! Zero! It is not yet noon, and yet you have already handed me the distinguisher between the self and the world while King Two approaches from a distance! The self is the self-aware unit of interactive thoughts thinking about the distinction between the world and the self. Surely not all interactive units of energy are conscious units of energy. Thus, the self is the only truly known consciousness in the world.

Zero: Is it, though?

One: Well, yeah. Other consciousnesses… conscii? Other conscii may be a deception of some elaborate programming. But you cannot be deceiving your own self-awareness.

Zero: Consciousnesses was the correct word. And we discussed this concept briefly yesterday, but didn't quite get into it. But wouldn't the solipsist rebut that the other consciousnesses, which you admit cannot be known for certain, may just as well be a simulation of your self-conscious phenomena as well?

Two: Good noon, gentleman. Zero, why do you bring up solipsism again? Such a rubbish Worldview that proves Everything and Nothing, with unwarranted levels of skepticism and Nonsense all at once.

Zero: You said it yourself; it is a worldview that posits that the self may be the totality of the world. And One and I were just discussing, (as I'm sure you already know, Two), that within the hypothesis that the world is capable of reasoning like the self, there is but a single axiom that affirms solipsism, namely, that the world is the self as being the totality of interactive energy.

Two: Zero, One, let me ask you a question. Are you omniscient?

One: Of course not, my Lord!

Zero: We would be fools to posit such a falsehood!

Two: Well, I am. The way I perceive you is merely a minimalist representation of the total possible perceptions of you. But the way I know you in my omniscient concept space is exactly as you are in real space. Therefore, solipsism can only be a valid worldview for God, Two, and others like us. But even we can distinguish our thoughts from the world, even when they look identical. It's merely a matter of scope.

Zero: Forgive me, my Lord, but you forget the possibility of a solipsist also believing in perpetual incompleteness which would also solve their lack of omniscience and also affirming their solitary worldview.

Two: YOU DARE QUESTION ME?! Have you no fear? Completeness is found Everywhere in the Worlds of logic and reality! The unit itself is complete in its unity. There could not be 2 units if 1 unit was never completed to begin with! To do otherwise would be to go back on the allowances you gave yesterday, and de-objectify the unit once again.

One: Well, there can still be units within incomplete units. Wouldn't this still be allowable for Zero's supposition? Objectify the subunits of things, all the while allowing the totality to be incomplete?

Two: But to make such an allowance would negate me, the omniscient one, as a valid entity! And I'm telling you; *there is completeness to my thoughts and knowledge.*

Zero: Sure, you're valid in concept space as an interactive thing of energy, but that doesn't mean that you're valid in real space. Just like the word 'words' being communicated in every way all at once is nonsense, but doesn't apply to reality, my Lord's complete science may also be nonsense to reality when it is demonstrated in its totality.

Two: Of course, it looks like Nonsense *to you*, but I can pick out every distinguished bit of knowledge within the totality and make sense of it all. Do you not remember yesterday, when you broke a smile at the absurdity of the supposition of the part implying the whole, and vice versa?

Zero: I do, my gracious purple haze. And it proved itself to be a necessary supposition, indeed, to progress beyond nonsense. Wait a second; you weren't there yet, Two! How did you know that I smiled?

Two: You've already deduced that for there to be a World, to begin with, its Energy must be complete and Non-negatable. In reality, I am the completeness of Energy itself. I am the completeness of the World. I am the whole Unit, and you are a part of the whole Unit. Not even Nothing itself can separate you from the Unit of my Kingdom. We imply each other, and your conscious Unity is a reflection of my own.

Zero: I… I did not expect that.

One: The King is very wise.

Zero: Even if the completeness of energy isn't conscious in the real world, it is certainly complete by itself.

One: Thus, any positing of incompleteness to the totality of energy of the real world is absolutely false.

Zero: Agreed.

One: Since reason requires a world to operate in, it *needs* energy to underlie it.

Zero: Yes, we already agreed to that yesterday. Why are you bringing it up again?

One: Mostly to drive this point into your thick skull, Zero. A logical system that affirms the energy it is based on *and* contains all the energy of the world with it *and* is aware of the concept of the Nothingness that is beyond the logical system would necessarily be a *complete* logical system, similar to the one inside Two's head.

Two: Even my representation in our peculiar Worlds of appearances demonstrates the possibility, from your perspective, and the certainty from my perspective, that such a logical system does not need to take the entirety of the World's Energy to be complete.

Zero: If you say so…

One: So a logical system that has clearly defined axioms and considers exceptions to the rule within the same axiom and a single Non-axiom for the axiom of Nothingness beyond and within the system, the system would be definitionally complete. I call this… the completeness theorem!

Zero: Just because you define something to be complete, doesn't mean that it actually is.

One: But without completeness, the individual axioms themselves within any logical system could never be posited to begin with.

Two: Yes, and the completeness of the part of the system implies the completeness of the whole, even if it has yet to be completed in Time. Your capacity is merely inadequate at the moment. Though I admit, a valid and interpretable information system can still be incomplete even within the completeness of the Energy system.

Zero: Fine! Let us grant that the completeness theorem is just as sensible as the incompleteness theorem. What would this imply about the self?

One: Only that there is a limit to the self, both in definition and capacity to the 2nd layer of energy to a thing. And that these things are completable.

Zero: I guess this 2nd layer of energy needs a thinking self to be known or observed. Or at least a processor of 1st layer energy pre-determined to fire a certain output regarding the 2nd layer determination.

Two: I am Lord over all concept Spaces. I am the one who pre-determines your outputs. I am Two; the God of Logics; and Provider of your capacity.

Zero: Or, now here's a thought, we evolve our capacity over generations and over time individually, and determine our outputs over time.

One: Maybe like a self-nature versus self-nurture kind of thing? A little bit of both?

Zero: Since when did you decide to be the middleman between Zero and Two, One?

One: …

Zero: OK, fine, that was a bad dad joke. But I agree, it's a little bit of both.

Two: No! It is all Nature! Your ability to adapt to different environmental circumstances in various capacities is itself programmed into your Nature! Nature and nurture are not different sets, nurture is simply a subset of Nature. *Nature is the World too.*

One: But according to our description of a thing, with its primary and secondary energies, wouldn't the nurtured behaviors be a part of the secondary energy, and thus be viewed as growing beyond nature?

Zero: Hmmm, I see what you mean, but that would imply that the secondary energy is supernatural or otherwise metaphysical, which I'm skeptical of. How would you solve this, Two?

Two: I already did, you moron! In response to your question, One, a thing's secondary Energy starts within and is limited by its Primary Energy. It is still metaphysical, yes, but it is still connected to its physical thingness in the real World.

Zero: What about the case of Everything physical? Can its secondary energy grow beyond itself?

One: No, I don't think so. All of Mass-Electric-Space-Time has all that it needs to contain its own secondary energy, having No-thing and No-energy beyond itself.

Two: Correct.

Zero: But what about the secondary energy of No-thing?

Two: There is None. But the secondary Energy of Nothing is Everywhere. The Primary Energy of Nothing is Vacuum Energy, and the secondary Energy of Nothing is the Nully Spirit.

Zero: Ramen to that.

One: So Two, does this mean that in a vacuous concept space itself, without appealing to the electromagnetic radiation underlying it, could hold the entirety of a thing's secondary energy? Could such a concept space hold the things in-themselves?

Two: Where else could it be, other than Nowhere? And it is there, since Nothing is in-itSelf in the real World. Hear my words, you two, a thing in-itSelf is a paradox. It assumes its own Unity, as we saw yesterday, a thing is a solitary Unit. But to be in-itSelf, it would require at least a 2nd Self, including the thing that is the Self's container, and the thing that is *inside* the container. Even when a thing is all by itSelf, there is still the Non-Self of Nothing by it, in the Perfect Vacuum World, acting as the container. The first layer of Energy is its container, being the Unit of the totality of Energy and the 4 Dimensions that are composed within it. The second layer of Energy works the same way to be its own container, being the Unit of the totality of the thing, and it is also the many Dimensions that comprise the thing, which could only ever happen in a conscious concept Space, in a Self, and explained Qualitatively.

One: That makes a good quantity of sense.

Zero: Hey! That sounds like a dimension to me, that seems like a good place to start today's scrimmage. How do you propose we measure the sensibility differences between different selves in the world of question? How can we know Two is reasonably telling us the truth, and not trying to deceive us?

One: You may have just answered your own question, Zero. For what is more reasonable than the truth of the matter? And how else can we prove what is true other than testing it?

Zero: I mean, a lot of falsehoods can be created to sound more reasonable than the truth, if the truth is complicated, but that doesn't matter for what we're doing if we do indeed go about testing the propositions being told. For instance, is there a distinction between the truths discovered in a thing's first layer of energy, and a thing's secondary layer? It seems that truth requires either a qualitative aspect to be proclaimed or an objective aspect to be tested.

One: As well as a quantitative aspect to define the magnitude of precision of the objective aspects being tested for sensibility.

Zero: I suppose so. Nebulous thinking, when defined as such, should be less sensible than precision of thought. But again, what distinguishes a true precise thought from an askew precise thought?

One: Wouldn't it be defined by its predefined definition reflecting the relevant energy dimensions in question?

Zero: But what makes the energy dimensions *in-themselves* truthfully precise?

One: The energy of the totality of the thing in question, naturally.

Zero: But that alone is a nebulous thought, is it not? It would require a re-appealing to its dimensional composition to make the notion precise again, and yet, we have by no means determined that it is the correct precise notion in-itself.

One: Well, shoot, you're right. Then it would follow that even truth cannot be true in-itself without appealing to energy again. Now the question goes, can we save truth by predefining that energy is true in-itself?

Zero: I'm afraid not. For we have already equated energy to the world of appearances, which was indeed necessary. Yet we cannot dismiss the truth of the impossibility to prove that appearances are not a deception. A world is there, sure, but we cannot know if it is a true or a false world.

One: Hmm, I think I felt a sprinkle.

Zero: But I believe Two and I agree from our perceptions, that it was a false sprinkle.

One: Don't gaslight me, Zero, I know a raindrop when I feel it! What a wretched proposition, a false sprinkle!

Two: You did and you did not feel a sprinkle. This is the Truth. Only from your perspective, it is beginning to rain, One. How could you feel a sprinkle absolutely without rain in our domains as well?

Zero: Now that you mention it, yeah, I do feel a bit of Non-rain pouring on me.

Two: Silence, you false schizo, no you do not. But that does raise a good point, One. Since we cannot verify your feelings and your sensations, besides an appeal to my omniscient ability to verify you, all others are, unfortunately, valid in their skepticism until they feel a sprinkle, near in Space and Time. Since Zero and I's concept Spaces have no water in them, we can conclude that all sensations in concept Space are false.

One: I see what you mean, my king. So am I correct to assert that truth can only be validated absolutely by the omniscient, but from our finite perspectives, truth is *relative* to its energy, not equivalent to it?

Two: Correct.

Zero: See? Truth includes our attempts to define what exists in the world other-than-I that is part of the energy in-total. That, and the energy in me.

One: So we're only left with relativistic truths to define the sensible energy dimensions in ourselves? A perfect storm is a-brewing now.

Zero: Hmmm, the brightness of your light *is* decreasing a bit, One. Don't feel down, making our definitive truths more precise is part of the fun of it. For me, anyway, defining the sensible energy dimensions is fun.

One: I guess. But where can I even start? If there is one thing I can forecast, it is that the world's energy dimensions can hold water because they define real objective things. But the psychological dimensions are defining subjective things from the start. If I say "Is X a dimension of the self?," even a novice skeptic could negate it since there isn't an objective thing to connect the designated attribute to!

Zero: I would loathe to negate you now whilst my victory is so near within reach. But what if we gave these hot pink poles a bit of life, and the ability to act amongst us, each other, and the world? We made them non-applicable quantitative units yesterday, perhaps we could make them non-applicable qualitative units today. *Or maybe some mannequins would be better…*

One: So, just focus on the behaviors in the world?… that could work! Let's spawn the pieces needed in a 3-way hexagonal chess board, but instead of playing chess, we can define certain behaviors the pieces could do.

Two: And if all the Living pieces and ourSelves could perform certain actions, it is describing a secondary Energy Dimension of a Thing, which, in this case, is describing the Self. If only certain special pieces can do certain things, it is either a gift, talent, disorder, or disability.

Zero: Seems reasonable. But this could become very chaotic very quickly if we don't focus on 1 piece in relation to all the other pieces. Focus on a white pawn. What could they do?

One: Well, it could do nothing. Just stand there, in line, in order, amidst their teammates.

Zero: That could mean a lot of things, though. And the pawn might not even understand their motivations to be stagnantly complacent and ready for battle at the will of another. Even if they were self-aware of their motivations, and we ask them what their motivations are, what they say could be a deception. They may also change their answers based on who is asking.

One: Shoot, you're right. Even the behaviors I could observe my pawn performing could be a deception by the pawn. So unreliable it all seems!

Two: For this exercise, you must assume the actions performed are genuine and True. You are exploring the True Self, not the masks a Self may put on. Every mask is the imitation of an alternative Self the individual wishes to convey, and must reflect a real Self to be convincing and not arouse suspicion or ambiguity.

Zero: So can a self genuinely be doing nothing? Not unless they're dead, I'm betting. Or fainting, frozen in terror, or asleep. I guess it depends on what you mean by *doing nothing.*

One: I probably meant being aware whilst immobile.

Zero: … Is *being* a way of behavior?

One: More likely, it's the self's secondary energy *being turned on.*

Zero: So awareness, and this conscientiousness, isn't a dimension of the self-world, but the *extent* of the self-world in-itself?

One: No, I think it's still a factor. It's like the more aware the pawn is, the clearer their perception of the world will be. Both their literal actions and mental worldview would be sharper, their ideas crisp, and their actions more controlled.

Zero: An interesting assessment. The vividity of a self-aware concept space. But don't allow me to put words in your mouth. One, please, tell me what you think awareness is.

One: Is it not perceptual concern for a fact, situation, or development of one's surroundings whilst being awake?

Zero: I think we could do better. Being awake is implied within concern, and the development of one's surroundings just sounds like the world as we defined it.

One: Is awareness the perceptual concern for a fact or situation in the world of concern?

Zero: It may not be. At first glance; this seems very similar to our definition of electric, which I remind you to be the totality of sensible appearances of points of contact. But I suppose we did make the distinction between sensibilities and perceptions then… I do wonder if clarifying its function as a capacity is a necessary one.

One: Is awareness the capacity for perceptual concern for facts within and about the world of concern?

Zero: More like the capacity for *accurate* perceptions within the world of concern.

One: Good, then. So my pawn had awareness. And they are otherwise doing nothing. Do all of our pieces possess some level or quantity of awareness?

Zero: They would have to be in order to be a genuine self to investigate, I suppose. But what would you propose a unit of awareness to be?

One: Probably a single accurate perception in the world.

Zero: But hypothetically speaking, what if your pawn cannot accurately perceive anything?

One: In that case, the pawn would have the quantity of 0 awareness. It is still some quantity and is distinct from having some non-applicable awareness. But having 0 awareness seems unlikely to achieve, even for a pawn.

Zero: Is it possible to have a negative quantity of awareness? Because as you just posited for 0 awareness, having -1 awareness is still some quantity, right?

One: I see your point… I would then clarify that the awareness score would need to be some *testable* quantity. One can receive a 0 on a test, but for any reasonably fair grader, a negative value on such a test would be a logically impossible feat.

Zero: That's acceptable for awareness, but is this applicable to every dimension of the self?

One: What do you mean, exactly?

Zero: I mean, just on the top of my head, what if we're trying to assess how useful or helpful your pawn will be to put either mine or Two's king into checkmate? To me and my black king, my pawn could be harmful to me if they choose to step out of line. And your queen could prove herself very harmful indeed. Wouldn't you agree that a positively helpful thing, a neutral useless thing, and a negatively harmful thing would all be a part of the same useful dimension?

One: Maybe? But maybe not, if the things can be all three at once depending on what the thing is going to be useful for… It certainly wouldn't be inherent to the thing itself. We'll have to wait and see if there is such a negative dimension of the self.

Zero: Fair enough. So One, let's move your pawn. Or rather, let it do things. What do you propose your pawn to do?

One: Oh boy, so many options! It can jump! It can ride on horseback with the knights! It can run to the center of the field! It can learn things! It could try everything! I see it now, Zero! This internal motivation to go out and try things is also a part of the self! The desire to not want to just sit around and do nothing!

Zero: Hmmm, it might not be just that. Even if a self does end up doing nothing, this attribute of the self we are observing would also be open to things being done to them just as well. That is the case unless they have a near 0 quantity of this attribute. If a 0 is even possible…

One: Even in this rain, I smile at the thought of such an obstinate self only being found by their unwillingness to take such a test in the first place.

Zero: Yes, it seems for this dimension, taking the test itself could be a non-zero unit of what it is trying to measure. That could potentially be problematic. What would you say this dimension is?
One: Is it openness to experience? That's what the psychologists say it is.
Zero: Perhaps, but is there a better word that encapsulates it?
One: Is it uninhibitedness? Lightheartedness? Or abandonment? Or naturalness?
Zero: Uninhibitedness doesn't encapsulate being receptive to actions being done to themselves. Abandonment, as well as naturalness, are ambiguous in English, at least. Lightheartedness is too emotionally based because it's like a reduction in mass that would otherwise inhibit the self from experiencing things, just like heavy heartedness is linked to sadness.
One: You know? After hearing you say that, I wonder if we may have been looking at this dimension backward. What if the more heartedness one has, the more energy has to be put in to be willing to experience things?
Zero: Again, it's not the heartedness, but the openness and the willingness. To treat this dimension like mass, and flip our perspective on it, then the better word to use would be reluctance.
One: And a unit of reluctance would be a thing a self is unwilling to do in relation to the circumstances. Then too much reluctance would be like the self being a black hole singularity where you cannot even test and see what's going on within the black hole if they are indeed reluctant to take the test.
Zero: What, then, is reluctance?
One: Is it a lack of willingness or desire to do or accept something?

Zero: Well, we cannot define this dimension by what it is not, or by what it is lacking. If we are comparing reluctance to mass, and mass is the totality of resistance to changes of action, what is reluctance? One more time.

One: Is it the capacity to resist changes of actions within the world of concern?

Zero: Not exactly, because this definition is limited by its mass. Reluctance is completely in the mind of the self.

One: Then is it the capacity to *mindfully* resist changes of action within the world of concern?

Zero: Yes, I believe it is. And we can also say that openness to experiences is the capacity to mindfully *affirm* changes of action within the world of concern. But this specification may not be necessary.

One: So my pawn is aware, and has a generalized preference to either accept or resist unfamiliar alterations to their world. I wonder if there is a similar dimension for preferring familiar patterns in the world.

Zero: Every familiar pattern to a self had to have been unfamiliar at some point in the past. So unless you'd like to assert that there exist innately familiar patterns that can be known apart from experience, I would think a preference for familiarity would correlate greatly for a self with a lot of reluctance.

One: And I would not make such an assertion, I see your point. Then perhaps we should look into how the pawn tends to alter their world.

Zero: Wouldn't such tendencies be more a part of the world and not a part of the self?

One: Like we said yesterday, all worlds have some things in common that are necessary to make it a world. But similar selves interacting with these common things in different worlds would produce similar behaviors whilst being distinct from reluctance. For example, in the real world, different fundamental particles can have different masses, but with similar spins. I'm proposing, in essence, that we dimensionalize this spin-of-the-self next.

Zero: Sure, why not? But… uh… what is *spinning,* exactly?

One: I'm dizzy just thinking about it. There can even be different spins along different axes that make completely new vectors for the self to be spinning along.

Zero: No… One, it's not the spatial axes we are defining but the spinning in-itself within the self. Like an inner angular momentum.

One: Just intuitively, it feels like a self with less spin would be pretty chill and laid back, while a self with a fast spin would be more uppity and…

Zero: *Neurotic!*

One: Yes. A fitting metaphor, is it not?

Zero: Kind of. If the metaphor is to fit completely, there should be an oppositely charged spin to the self.

One: What do you mean by that?

Zero: I mean, there should be a distinction between a self that is spinning clockwise or counterclockwise. If this is accurate, the metaphor fits, but we will need to explore what this counter-neuroticism is. If not, the metaphor is an incomplete shadow of a representation of the self.

One: So is there an anti-neuroticism that would cancel out neuroticism if they came in contact with one another? An excellent question! Two, care to share your thoughts?

Two: Every particle has an antiparticle. The antiparticle properties in the Self have opposite charges and opposite spins. However, from the Self's point of reference, spinning is spinning and feels identical most of the Time. Neuroticism is driven by unprovoked fear and anxiety, and its counterpart of Irritability is driven by unprovoked disgust, anger & loathing. But when they are brought together in the World, balanced, their Self-Energies cancel out. All spins can be Quantified positively, but you will do best to define Neuroticism positively and Irritability negatively, to give this Dimension of the Self completeness.

Zero: Cool. I guess we'll look into the charge of the self later. But for now, what word would you propose could encapsulate these two extremes, One?

One: Sensitivity? Reactionary, maybe? Responsiveness?

Zero: No, no, no, these are all still concerning the world! We need something like inner sensitivity, and overreacting to possibilities contained within a self's concept space that are not yet actualized in the world.

One: Like intuition? Or instinct, perhaps? Visceral? Edginess?

Zero: Intuition and instinct have been overused, and come with a bit of baggage. Visceralness? Hmmm, I think it's too medical. But edginess, as a positive iteration of uneasiness, being defined by both irritability and anxiety… it's the ideal word.

One: I'm sure the neurotics of the world would take kindly to being labeled Edge Lords instead of neurotic.

Zero: Neurotic would still apply to around half of the Edge Lords. But I agree, it ironically takes the edge off the label to be labeled edgy. But what is edginess?

One: Is it the capacity to maintain anxious or irritable tension in a precarious, unstable, and restless mental state?

Zero: That seems like mental disequilibrium to me.

One: I suppose it is.

Zero: How does that make sense in the colloquial sense? How can anything maintain instability?

One: Here is an example. As you can see, the objects of our pawns have rounded tops. It makes it very difficult to balance or stabilize things on top, but not impossible. So when we stack our pawns on top of each other, would I be in error to suggest that my pawn on the bottom is maintaining an unstable position for the other pawns?

Zero: From your pawn's perspective, that is as stable as they can be!

Two: Yes, but from any of our rook's perspectives, who would no doubt provide greater support to any other piece, One's pawn should not be bearing the weight of their king all on their own. It would take 3 pawns close together to stabilize what 1 rook can do alone. On top of a single pawn, a single movement or gust of wind would expose the pawn's instability for what it is. A lot of potentially disastrous shifting from potential to kinetic Energy from both the first and second layers can emerge.

Zero: Sigh, I get it now…

One: See, it's not the position of the other pawns that makes my pawn unstable, but the roundness of its top that demonstrates its instability, and that roundness is itself maintained. The pawn can train itself to become more level-headed like the rook, but they don't have to. And if they don't train themselves to reach equilibrium, and remain stagnant in this form of growth, we can then say that they maintain their instability.

Zero: A fully adequate demonstration for me! But edginess should still be defined more simply…

One: How about this? Edginess is the capability to maintain mental instability with anxiety and/or irritation.

Zero: Or maybe the capacity to be mentally *disturbed* with anxiety and/or irritation. *Instability* may have been the better word to use at first in the examples above, but I'm pretty sure it is their inner *disturbances* that ultimately drive their *instability.*

One: Perfect. Now we can explore the idea of the charge of the self.

Zero: How will this differ from awareness at all?

One: A great amount. About as different as a photon is different from a neutron. But what is it?

Two: I'll give you a hint. The two of you are opposite charges of the same person.

Zero: The same person? But our perceptions are completely different!

One: I agree with Zero. If we are of the same person, then which of us holds the true charge of the person?

Two: Both of you hold the true charge. Neither of you are fake in this regard. Your common person holds a neutral charge, fully accepting his anima and animus. One is anima, Zero is animus, and I am Ego, with a bit of extra knowledge added in.

Zero: A bit? Two, how large is our common person's ego to claim he is just a few bits of knowledge shy of being omniscient?

Two: In a sense, I do know Everything as being the totality of Units of Energy and the total subjective Dimensional analysis of the totality of Units. Everything is simply the totality of Things, and even you two discovered what a Thing is yesterday.

One: It is a troll's answer, but it's not wrong either. Perhaps the king's large ego is justified?

Zero: No, it is not! My dear One, it is our duty to keep Two's sense of self in check! Like a couple of wise men guiding their king in matters of the king's mind. We don't merely fight *for* him in times of war, but *with and against* him in matters of truth and wisdom. A false ego is never justified, and any king worth his salt will be open to correction from his loyal allies.

Two: Zero, are you loyal to me?

Zero: What fool would be disloyal to themselves? Of course, I am loyal.

One: I think those people whose animus seizes their ego would be justified if their ego was adequately demonstrated to be in error from even their anima's perspective.

Zero: When Two is as wise as he is, he has nothing, not a single thing to fear from his shadow. We make him even stronger, One. That is my stance.

Two: A good answer, indeed.

Zero: Still, what exactly is this opposing charge between us, One? If it could be summarized into a single word, what would it be?

One: Can it even be condensed into a single dimension?

Zero: We already contrasted the negative aspects between us. I'm more of an irritable edginess, and you are more of a neurotic edginess. It's not that pronounced in either of us, but it is there.

One: But our relative aspects of anima and animus are strong. You're rational, wise, and objective in sticking to the facts. I'm compassionate, loving, and considerate of all forms of life. But what word encompasses this dichotomy between truth and love? Care? Godliness? Sincerity? Honesty? Dutifulness? Virtue?

Zero: Not godliness… Sincerity and honesty are too focused on the truth side… Dutifulness is an effect of *whatever this is*, I think. Care and virtue are pretty close. Don't tell me this is either ethicality or morality!

One: So a moral compass is a part of the self, huh? Not beyond. What could be more ethical than sticking to what is loving and what is true?

Zero: I cannot contemplate an answer to that. Save for a morality offered by an omniscient and omnibenevolent entity. Or at least defer moral judgments to those with a greater capacity for love and truth. But I wouldn't throw out the possibility of morality beyond the self, for what is loving, much like truth, should be falsifiable, replicable, and judged via peer review.

One: What a novel idea, Zero! And rather romantic, as well.

Zero: Eh, not really. We test love over time all the time, and consider it genuine when it endures. But never mind all this, and let's get to defining it. One, what is the dimension of morality, as far as the self is concerned?

One: Is it the capacity to distinguish between right and wrong, and/or between good and bad actions in the world of concern?

Zero: Hmmm, you know what, this is a first. The definition is better than the word we're trying to define! I realize that morality is more about the end product of the ethical judgments; the code of ethics determined. The word we should be using should be focusing on the judging process itself, not the outcome of the judgments.

One: Good catch! Shall we use *discernment* instead?

Zero: Fine by me.

One: And would you agree that discernment is the capacity for accurate and/or ethical judgments of actions within the world of concern?

Zero: I believe I would agree, but I do have a small concern we should cover. What meaningfully distinguishes discernment from awareness? I mean, if you accurately perceive a thing through awareness, wouldn't that imply an accurate judgment of the perception has already occurred?

One: A very concerning question! But allow me to explain, I do believe I have an answer. Awareness in-itself makes no judgments. It is aware of things to concern itself with, and that's all! It concerns the clarity of the initial perception, which, for example, can make my pawn appear more crisp or blurry as an object or idea. Discernment is distinct from awareness in this way. Let's say my pawn has a blurry awareness of your pawn, but a strong, accurate, and ethical judgment concerning the actions your pawn performs. The discernment comes after awareness and is a completely different process in the mind of the self.

Zero: OK, but that brings up a different problem. If discernment comes after awareness, wouldn't that make discernment a lesser, secondary dimension to the self that requires awareness of a thing primarily before making a judgment on it?

One: When you get pedantic about it, you could say reluctance and edginess are also secondary to awareness in this way, and that only awareness is *necessary* for a self. But because these processes can operate simultaneously, even though at some point in the past awareness came first, they are equally fundamental in the present.

Zero: So would you say that awareness comes first causally, but as a function of the self, they run independently of each other?

One: Kind of. I'm not denying the causal link, but I am saying that we can use discernment now to judge that discernment and awareness are different categories that we can use to measure the self at a fundamental level when we currently observe it.

Zero: So awareness involves perceiving a thing in an instant, in 1 Now, and discernment involves attributing the various qualia over many Nows via interconnective thought?

One: There would be no qualia without discernment. And we've already agreed that the total subjective dimensional analysis of the energy is a key defining part of what a thing is.

Zero: Good point. In that case, and with the need for qualia in mind, I am satisfied with the distinction. Awareness perceives the world, and discernment distinguishes differences between things in the world.

One: Not just differences, but similarities, patterns, and inferences too.

Zero: Indeed. Now then! Are there any other charge-like dimensions within our anima and animus dichotomy?

One: Just to name a few possibilities: patient and headstrong, creative versus destructive, vanity and simplicity, feminine and masculine, subject and object, extrinsic versus intrinsic…

Zero: Woah there, Mr. Sparky, must we explore and consider every single dichotomy to see if it applies to the self?! A lot of your examples don't seem inherent. Love and truth as modes of discernment, sure, but wouldn't it make sense if patience correlates with some combination of reluctance and discernment in some way?

One: Hmmm… yes, I see what you mean. Which ones are fundamental, and which ones are emergent? I think it would be best tackled by returning to focus on my pawn's actions amid the world. It has awareness, reluctance as a will against certain actions, edginess to react to stimuli, and discernment to differentiate beneficial from harmful stimuli. Wouldn't giving the self a general sense of will *for* certain actions make sense? Like motivation or desire?

Zero: Yes, that offers us a much better explanation of the patience/headstrong dichotomy as well! Patience is low reluctance

& low desire for anything else, while headstrong is high reluctance & high desire for something else!

One: Motivation is not quite a charge, though. You either have it or you don't; there is no negative motivation.

Zero: Are you sure? Wouldn't punishment be, as you call it, a negative motivation?

One: Regarding the actions in the world, sure, punishment is a negative motivation, but regarding the self?… Hmmm… I guess we need the self to have the will to avoid certain states in the world of concern.

Zero: Without some aversion to harm, selves with low reluctance wouldn't live very long. On the other hand, when we give the self negative motivations, the self would then be capable of punishing itself for reasons as mundane as simply existing.

One: King Two, what is the solution to this dilemma? Do we allow selves with low reluctance to be mindfully accepting of an avoidable death? Or do we allow selves the capacity to have high negative & self-punishing motivation that could mindfully move the self towards a premature death?

Two: Clearly, it is the second option that is in line with reality. Having low Reluctance or high Openness to Experience may lead the Selves to perform more risky behaviors, but their Motivations to do risky things can range from an incentivizing dopamine rush to having an active death wish against themSelves. Even still, a Will to desire specific positive states or actions in the World is required for a Self to seek their Equilibrium. It is better to admit that a Will to death is a possible byproduct of having a Will than it is to remove a Will to Live by negating a Will altogether.

Zero: Here, hear, the king speaks the truth! So a self requires motivation to be valid. What would you say motivation is, One? Or is motivation even the best word to use here?

One: I think it is the best word. Maybe intrinsic motivation would be better, but seeing that even extrinsic motivation cannot function without a self, it's probably good as it is. Desire, will, and determination have more issues, I think.

Zero: Yeah, none of those hit the punishment/reward dichotomy as well. Perhaps the word 'will' does, but it's too ambiguous in English. Carry on, then…

One: Is motivation the capacity to desire and/or avoid things within the world of concern?

Zero: Almost… Well… actually… yeah, it is. I was going to suggest adding *particular* things, but then I remembered that desires and avoidances can be generalized as well. I still kind of wish it could accentuate the reasoning behind the desires and avoidances, but that may not apply to all selves.

One: That should be fine. It's not the actualized amount of the dimension of the self that we are currently concerned about. Only that the self holds the capacity to hold a Non-Zero quantity as a part of its secondary energy.

Zero: Hopefully putting a 0 in one or more of these dimensions of self doesn't negate them. It would be a shame if someone were to do that. Ha ha, can you imagine what a self that holds a 0 in every dimension of the self except in edginess would look like?

One: What an odd tangent to go on, Zero. And of course, you would bring up the most sadistically tortured self imaginable. Do these torturous tests on your own pawns, and leave mine out of it! It's possible in this concept space, but in the real world, the odds of this happening to a real self are slim to none.

Zero: True enough. Ok, I'll back off, it was just a funny thought…
Now, of the dichotomies you've already mentioned, the only two
that sparked my interest were vanity and simplicity, and feminine
and masculine, so let's focus on those. One, would you state that
the capacity to be materialistic is *inherent* to the self?
One: When you put it that way, no, I don't think so. The self is
emergent from the material, as being less necessary than the world.
Plus, it appears too closely connected to reluctance as it is.
Zero: Well, that was fast. And what of the other dichotomy?
One: Not to intentionally posit an appeal to emotion, but I think
either position could be counted as an insult or in error. If we say
the dimension of gender is a part of the self, we would risk
removing a major factor of the worldly energy of the brain and
body affecting the self entirely. It would insult any reasonable
person to say there is no correlation between masculinity and
having a Y chromosome at all. Then again, major deviations do
still occur. Perhaps these deviations can be accounted for with
these other dimensions of the self.
Zero: Hmmm, I suppose men do tend to be more irritably edgy,
and women more anxiously edgy. Masculine individuals also tend
to be more detail-oriented in their discernments, while feminine
individuals have caring orientations in their discernments. So do
we agree that gender isn't fundamental to the self?
One: I believe we do… What else is there? What about memory?
Zero: I don't think so. Memory is a learning process that applies to
awareness and discernment over spans of time within the world of
concern.
One: Wow, you are shooting my propositions down fast now! OK,
OK, what about introversion and extraversion?!

Zero: You mean high reluctance coupled with a low motivational desire for most other selves?

One: … Wow… Fine. And agreeableness?

Zero: Even a Zero with minimal awareness and discernment could see agreeableness as low reluctance with high motivation to either desire equilibrium and/or avoid disequilibrium with others, often to counterbalance their high edginess.

One: It does seem that for all actions in the world of concern, and all behavior driven by the self can be awareness, reluctance, discernment, motivation, and edginess.

Zero: Hold it… I think I see something… We realized that we needed motivation. But the more I look at it, it seems that reluctance is a subset of motivation.

One: That's a bold move. Care to elaborate?

Zero: Well, in the mind of a self, could we not reduce the "charges of actions" into a single dimension? When we treat actions as possible-active-things-in-itself, reluctance mindfully resists changes of action, and can be reworded to be indistinguishable from motivation, as its capacity to mindfully avoid these things-of-action.

One: … Reluctance *is* an expression of the will, isn't it?

Zero: Exactly.

One: So all behaviors of my pawn can be reduced to being capable of sensing and perceiving as awareness, being capable of judging one thing from another as discernment, and being capable of willfully desiring one thing and avoiding another as motivation?

Zero: Reasonably speaking, I am content with this deduction. But this begs the question. Can edginess, as a sort of flavor-state a self can be in, be negated as well?

One: Or perhaps expanded.

Zero: Can edginess stand distinct from awareness of being in disequilibrium, as its judging of the self to be in disequilibrium, and its motivation to head the self towards equilibrium? And if so, can this self in disequilibrium be meaningfully distinguished from the self's first layer energy being in disequilibrium?

One: To answer your first question, the answer is clearly yes. Edginess is a state of being for the self. Self-awareness, self-discernment, and self-motivation are all distinct from the being-a-self or the self's state-of-being. The first three don't make the fourth. But your second question? Hmmm… Wouldn't this require an example of an object in equilibrium whose subject is in disequilibrium, or vice versa?

Zero: It would have to, I think.

One: To be certain, wouldn't we have to know the status of the totality of the object, or the subject to come to such a conclusion?

Zero: Not just any subject, but a self-aware subject.

One: Dang, this is impossible without appealing to the omniscient!

Zero: Be my guest, and good luck, One!

One: O omniscient Two, is it possible for an avatar to be in equilibrium while the self is in disequilibrium?

Two: Such a thing does not exist in any World but the empty Non-World, because avatars are always in motion, and perfect Equilibrium is thus impossible to maintain for an object in constant Energetic action for even a single Now.

One: O omniscient Two, is it possible for a self to be in equilibrium while the avatar is in disequilibrium?

Two: Yes.

Zero: Care to provide an example?

Two: I have 2 examples. A Self that is disillusioned with inaccurate Awareness and Discernment can still have inner peace.

Like the wise from generation's past say, "ignorance is bliss," and I add that blissfulness is found in states of Equilibrium. The second example is a Self that has learned to accept that the Equilibrium of the World cannot endure for longer than 1 Now before returning to Disequilibrium once again. Such a Self has accurate Awareness and Discernment of the World, and their Edginess is brought to Naught, and their Motivations are Selflessly minded towards the Equilibrium of Others.

One: You never cease to amaze me, Two! That gave me goosebumps!

Zero: No, it didn't.

One: Either way, do you question Two's perfect discernment?

Zero: Not as a negation, no. The capability for a self to be in equilibrium is indeed possible. Now I am wondering if mental disturbances are limited to just the anxiety and/or irritation of edginess, or if there are more.

One: Clearly, all that remains is the self's state of being to be concerned about. Perhaps we can view this problem musically. Just as a note or chord in tune is in equilibrium, and can negate its resonating by being sharp or flat, maybe we can see anxiety and/or irritation as sharp to the self and ask ourselves, *what is flat?*

Zero: Sadness, depression, unreactive… Huh? Now that you mention it, edginess is like a hyper-sensitive state of being, and it would make sense for a self to have a capacity for a hypo-sensitive state of being too.

One: Now we're talking!

Zero: Yet, what is edginess *and* flatness? Flatness can be combined with edginess under the self-dimension of disturbance or disequilibrium. So rather than categorizing the different kinds of mental disturbances, generalize all disturbances of the self as a capacity.

One: I suppose we could. I prefer disequilibrium personally, but disturbance may be the better word. And it is the capacity to be mentally disturbed. Full stop.

Zero: Eh, that's too close to using a word to describe the word it's describing. Let's make it the capacity to be mentally troubled and/or distracted, instead.

One: Good idea. Hmmm, are there any other flavors or kinds of states of being for the self? Maybe frequency or rhythm?

Zero: What an odd suggestion. Why frequency or rhythm?

One: We acknowledge that a self must be *being*. So the self is there as opposed to not being there.

Zero: And?

One: It made me think of a 1-dimensional space line being disturbed and creating a wave, and how else a wave can behave.

Zero: Well, both frequency and rhythm are measured with time. And disturbance in-itself is the amplitude, yes, I see that now. So all other flavors of the self would be derived from the self's first layer of energy, it seems.

One: Maybe we should presuppose an additional aspect of the self's state of being in order to find it. Currently, I'm imagining a well-rounded self of various magnitudes. A circle can be expressed as a wave, yet it is not a disturbance for the circle to have a greater or lesser amplitude, expressed as its radius.

Zero: You may be onto something… the only thing I can think to ask is if this well-rounded self could be expressed as a function of the other dimensions we've discussed thus far.

One: It's odd. In a way, it's like the capacity of the self-in-itself being actualized to the maximum amplitude which makes the self appear to take up a larger amount of space, without actually taking up more space.

Zero: Still, a self can be well-rounded without having reached its maximum possible amplitude.

One: Can it, though? A flat tire is a form of disturbance as… Well, flatness.

Zero: Yes, but with this analogy, it is the *size* of the tire we are concerning ourselves with, not its flatness. It's like the self is a living tire with the capacity to grow and expand its own radius, expanding the length of the self's perimeter. Although, in a sense, a disturbed self with 2 or 3 space-like dimensions would have a larger perimeter. So it's more like being efficient or adaptable, within a given capacity.

One: No, that would make well-roundedness a function of discernment when it's a state of being, not a status within the world of concern.

Zero: That's only a problem for you. I say that well-roundedness *is* a function of high discernment and low disturbance.

One: So we were onto nothing, it seems.

Zero: We learned a bit more. That's the value of it.

One: Then all that remains for a self is the inquiry into the self's actions being genuine or false in the first place. Like the self is there, but its actions can be made in pretense, or its state of being is not as it appears, like an illusion.

Zero: And you already admitted that truth and genuineness are relative to their energy, not equivalent to it.

One: I wouldn't jump to the conclusion just yet, Zero. A self can be truly genuine, falsely genuine, or truly fake. Even being falsely fake requires a genuine person to act fake.

Zero: So even a genuine person holds the capacity to deceive? How does this not make the self in question less genuine!?
Two: With high Discernment, a highly Genuine Self will know when to deceive. But Zero is right, my loyal One, just for the wrong reasons. Genuineness is a product of Motivation. It is a Will that desires acceptance from the Others and avoids being the cause of any Disturbance in Others. What emerges from such a Self is an honest, warm, and vulnerable individual, all from this aspect of Motivation.
One: My Lord, are you saying that a self is not genuine in-itself, but is motivated towards genuineness to get what they value?
Two: Correct.
One: Then would it not follow that genuineness is a thing to be valued, as an ideal state of being?
Two: Yes, but not all things are part of the Self Fundamentally. A Self that was Genuine and only Genuine would never be capable of Disingenuous acts, which would violate their Will to flee from that which they don't want, and to acquire that which they do want.
Zero: But doesn't this conflict with what you just said, when you said, "With high Discernment, a highly Genuine Self will know when to deceive," and "A Self that was Genuine and only Genuine would never be capable of Disingenuous acts." So which is it, Two?
Two: Listen to the words of Two! Genuineness is both a Virtue and a mode of action. Its Virtuousness stems from Discernment, and its actions in the World stem from Motivation. With low Discernment, a highly Genuine person (who is Motivated towards this) will have no choice but to commit Genuine acts. With low Motivation, a highly Genuine person (who Discerns it as a noble Virtue) will be capable of Disingenuous acts in whatever Will they have to act.

This is why Genuineness, and all Virtues, are not Fundamental to the Self, even though they emerge from the Self and are influenced by Others in the World.

Zero: Wow. I'm so glad I asked. I'm content with that answer.

One: Perhaps the virtues themselves, when applied, are what makes this well-roundedness of the self emerge into being.

Zero: That sounds right… it resonates. Questioning the validity of such a statement would be futile.

One: So is this the complete fundamental qualitative dimensions of the self? Is the self just a unit of interactive energy with the capacity to be aware, discerning, motivated, and disturbed by the world and/or itself?

Zero: Just a couple of minor tweaks. We should make the distinction between *a* self and *the* self. All other selves that are not *the* self are *an*other self.

One: Yes, it would be best to define a self, in this case, as any self-discerning self capable of recognizing that they were a self when adequately communicated with. So is a self a unit of energy with the capacity to be aware, discerning, motivated, and disturbed by the world of concern and/or itself?

Zero: Hmmm, the more I think about it, the more I'm convinced that it is not by the world of concern *and/or* itself that the whole self may be derived from its parts. My main point is that each part of the self *must* apply to itself in order to be a self. A self *must* hold the capacity to be self-aware, self-discerning, self-motivated, and self-disturbed. Therefore, a self is actually a unit of energy with the capacity to be aware of, discerning of, motivated by, and disturbed by the world of concern *and* itself.

One: Ah, yes! Great catch!

Two: This is close enough to be deemed correct.

One: Haha, do you see now why total self-negation is impossible, Zero? To become unaware is to be ignorant of all phenomena. To become discernless is to be a fool. To be unmotivated is to be dead inside, and to be undisturbable is to be unconcerned and uncaring about anything. To even deduce self-negation to have occurred requires the motivation to communicate that fact to be so and the discernment to be convinced by it in the first place.
Zero:…
One: Zero?
Zero:…
One: LOOK! BEHIND YOU! THERE IS A NEGATIVE ONE OVER THERE!
Zero:…
One: A solid quanta joke, and you cannot even provide me the slightest satisfaction?
Two: Zero, speak, or I will Genuinely negate you.
Zero: Fine. One, you are right. Until we enter the Great Nothingness that comes After, total self-negation is impossible. It could never reach our conscious awareness if it did, and it would be poor discernment to say it has happened already.
One: Thank you. Now, if we may, consider the parallels between the world and the self. The real world, as far as we can tell, has 4 primary dimensions comprising the totality of its energy. And the real self, we have just deduced, also has only 4 primary dimensions, comprising our capacity to exist. Also, as I now observe, each of the dimensions of the self corresponds to a dimension of the world, while being distinct from it. Motivation corresponds to mass, as desirable attractions reflect gravitational attractions, and avoiding repulsive things reflects mass' definitional resistance to changes of action. Awareness corresponds

to electric, as accurate perceptions within the world require light to sensibly appear to enlighten the self on the status of the world. Discernment can sort of be paired with space as a function to judge the distances and speeds of other objects in the world, even though it focuses more on the particular points of contact rather than the space between them. Plus, discernment can technically be made towards any dimension, so to single out space to correlate with it would be disingenuous. Disturbances can likewise sort of be paired with time, as a function of entropy, as the amount of disorder in an open system increases over time, but again, this is more focused on the collection of stuff within the system and not on time itself.

Zero: I mean… that's cool and all, but it doesn't add anything to what we said earlier.

One: It wasn't supposed to; it was just a summary with a post-qualitative data analysis of the results.

Zero: It's not exactly proper… but I'll allow it this time. It's true enough for an analysis, anyway. So… you called the world Mass-Electric-Space-Time, does this mean you'll call the self a Motivated-Awareness-Discerning-Disturbances?

One: Don't be silly, Zero, it would be M.A.D.D.-ness to do so!

Zero: Why so M.A.D.D., One, I thought you liked witty puns? I appeal to Two's judgment.

Two: Remember your deduction that these Dimensions must be applied to the Self to be a valid Self? It is not enough to be a Motivated-Awareness-Discerning-Disturbances, but the Self in question must be a Self-Motivated-Awareness-Discerning-Disturbances. A hyper-Aware Self can say of their own volition, "I am M.A.D.D."

One: Sigh… yes, my Lord… you are the M.A.D.D.est of them all, aren't you?

Two: Just in Awareness and Discernment, my loyal One. With these Dimensions alone, I know how to keep Disturbances to a minimum. It is you two who drive my Motivation to protect my kingdom. Without you, I often find myself too bored with Everything to act within it. But I already told you this…

One: True that.

Zero: That does raise a question, though. If omniscience negates motivations, wouldn't that negate the selfhood of the omniscient entity in question?

One: No, it doesn't negate the motivation, it just makes the motivational capacity of the omniscient self really low.

Two: Correct.

Zero: OK, ok, I was just asking. So… I guess we're done for today?

One: I did have one question in the back of my mind the whole time. It seems that, in general, I won today's battle. And yet, it is still raining in my concept space, after 4 groveling hours, nonetheless! Two, I thought this rain was foreshadowing something ominous and odious. So what gives? Why is it still raining?

Two: Sometimes, fictional rain is just rain with no deeper meaning. Your rain is just one of those mundane things that merely simulate phenomena of the real World. That is all.

Zero: Or maybe my victory tomorrow during our match will be absolute! I shall rise again on the 3rd day with my subjective morality pertaining to the other!

One: Oh, so you think. Not everything is permissively ethical under all circumstances. It'll just be a matter of adequately defining which things or actions are never ok.

Zero: Everything is acceptable under the right conditions.

Two: Except disobeying my orders, when my orders are verified to be reasonable. And now, hear my next order! We shall convene here in 12 hours! Bright and early at 4 a.m.! One shall bring the artificial Light sources, and Zero shall bring the Darkness that surrounds it, as well as the breakfast refreshments. Yes, Zero, bring some breakfast burritos.

Zero: I'll animate my pawns to prepare such a feast, my royal haziness.

Day 3: The Other

One: *yawns* *sniffs* MMM, that smells good. That should wake me up nicely.

Zero: I've been up since 1am. I went to sleep as soon as I got home to take a nap, then it just turned into a full-on sleep.

One: Lucky you. I could barely sleep. I was too excited over yesterday's victory and anxious for today's battle.

Zero: Here, have some coffee and a burrito. I hope you like it black.

One: I don't, actually, but it'll have to do, I suppose.

Zero: I'm just messing with you. There's sugar, stevia, creamer, and milk, too.

One: Bless you, Zero.

Zero: I think Two would have considered it a crime not to have any of that good white stuff available. We both know he likes to keep things balanced between our respective forces.

One: *sips* And speaking of crime, Zero, I believe that's an excellent topic to warm up with this morning. I believe that when we understand crime in its entirety, we will be capable of both combating and averting shame and guilt when there isn't something to feel ashamed or guilty of. And these things plague the self more often than not.

Zero: I hold zero shame, One. What is there to be ashamed of?

One: A lot of things! Things that disturb the collective equilibrium, mostly. And even some selfish equilibrium-seeking behavior is shameful.

Zero: Would you care to distinguish what exactly these selfish equilibrium-seeking actions are, so that we can determine where shame is valid or invalid? Where is this line drawn?
One: I think the actions that would disturb others' personal equilibrium would be the standard for shameful acts, would it not?
Zero: It depends on what you mean by *"personal equilibrium."* It could be a problem if you refer to another person's subjective and opinionated threshold for disgust, and not merely acts of objective disturbance. I should not be expected to feel shame for eating vegetables in front of a picky toddler, or the eggs in this breakfast burrito in front of a vegan.
One: That is a good point. Perhaps it is either the depreciation or disturbance of another's objective equilibrium we should be concerned with. Their subjective equilibrium is only validated when there is a clear depreciation at work in the world. Only when the depreciation is unclear does a self require discernment to judge the issues at hand.
Zero: Is the world ever so clear? The facts at hand concerning matters of the world may be a deception. *Especially* when others' motivations come into play.
One: What do you mean? Provide an example.
Zero: Suppose two of my pawns were to be hidden behind this tree we see. For some invalid reason, one hates the other and plans to assault them. They knock the other out cold, then proceed to do themselves harm to make the appeal of self-defense for their actions before me, their judge. To me, an outside observer, both stories between the pawns would appear valid and plausible, especially if the victim harbors some hatred towards the perpetrator, before or after the incident. Perpetrators of disturbance

are motivated to reduce a judge's awareness of the facts of the situation to sway their discernment in their own favor.

One: Another good point. It appears, if I am to make any progress in today's battle, I would need to assume perfect awareness of the situation for the judge to make an ethical judgment of the situation to execute proper justice.

Zero: We'll have to let Two decide. Perhaps my victory today is limited in the real world, where perfect awareness is impossible.

One: No, this matter goes hand-in-hand with the completeness theorem posited yesterday. Since the energy of the world is complete, and I am energy that is aware within the totality, then it follows that a self could hold a complete awareness of a system assigned to it, especially a simple system.

Zero: So we will have this debate in hopes that such a perfectly aware system may be available one day, and that future non-omniscient judges will create justice based on the system's data? Sounds like a dystopia to me.

One: And like a utopia to me.

Zero: Entropy would inevitably corrupt such a system. Therefore, it'd be a dystopia.

One: A perfect system would know how to correct such errors. Therefore, it'd be a utopia.

Two: Now that you are within earshot, Zero should grant One perfect Awareness of these hypothetical situations we are about to play out. Zero would annihilate One's army, and meet me in a stalemate if we were to have his way.

Zero: As you wish.

One: Thank you, my Lord. Now Zero, I did have this other concern on my mind. Are all selfish acts toward a personal equilibrium that harm or otherwise depreciate or disturb others' objective equilibrium, truly *shameful?*

Zero: Certainly not. There is always an exception to the rule, due to change given the circumstances.

One: Really? I figured the additive *"selfish"* would have made it crystal clear where shame starts and ends.

Zero: Not always; there are circumstances where an arbiter of justice must act quickly to ensure that less damage to others is done. Even still, it may yet be called *"selfish"* to enforce damage control when it's none of your business to begin with.

One: Hmmm, and it may just as well be labeled selfish to refrain from action entirely in such a scenario. The sensible way to resolve this problem would be to grant the arbiter the authority to intervene from the start.

Zero: That in itself may be an invalid appeal to authority. But I suppose we have already granted perfect awareness to all involved in the situation. Hmmm, but then again, a vigilante may perform justice, and be granted the authority after the fact to reinforce the right behavior within society. So if justice can be executed by anyone with adequate awareness, why does this arbiter need authority to intervene?

One: It's a matter of being validated, pre-approved, and reviewed within the perfectly aware system. That is all we have been granted by Two; the actors themselves don't need perfect awareness, and thus, as extensions of the perfectly aware system, need to demonstrate having a certain threshold of awareness and training how to discern properly to perform acts of justice within the system. And because the vigilante did not undergo this training and only acted on instinct, they should still feel shame in this case. Not a lot, but enough shame to cooperate with the pre-validated authorities at least, right?

Zero: Under a perfectly aware system, sure. But in the real world, unjust authorities who were pre-validated have performed many injustices. In this case, wouldn't the vigilante be justified to not cooperate with the authorities, if by chance the authority has horrible discernment?

One: I suppose they would. So yeah, I grant that the collective faith in the justice system would need to be granted before ordered justice could be reliably executed. It would be anarchy, otherwise.

Zero: Sounds good to me. In any case, whether or not this faith in the justice system is valid should always be up for debate. But amongst all this talk on authority, we have yet to define it.

Two: We can set up our pieces properly in the meantime.

Zero: Sounds great! OK, One, what is an authority?

One: It is a self in power over others in the world of concern.

Zero: Does it have to be a self? If your chess pieces were without a self, wouldn't your king and queen still hold authority over your pawns? And in the real world, couldn't a computer be an authority over a domain? Mankind gives authority to non-existent things as well, like gods.

One: I guess not… a hierarchy can exist without a self, like in the periodic table of elements, and be observed as a self-less other of varying magnitudes. In a sense, massive objects hold authority over their respective satellites and other lesser objects. However, we still need a self to observe the authoritative structure.

Zero: But that self does not need to be within the power system to observe it.

Two: Correct. However, adequate Awareness is incomplete when only viewed from outside the power system. Even from within, the dominated and the domineering will hold vastly different viewpoints, and how they interact can change vastly depending on the Selves involved. But if no Selves are involved in the hierarchy, the change in viewpoints does not affect the Energy structure overall.

One: Then should we choose another word besides authority to clarify that different motivational wills are involved?

Two: Authority is fine. It doesn't matter if you change the word to supervisor, management, government, power, or control. A Self can only be controlled as far as its avatar in the World is controlled. It is up to the Self, the avatar's situation in the World of concern, and how they will react to the powers that be. A strong Self filled with M.A.D.D.ness is difficult to handle, but they are also free. Within a State that truly endorses its liberty, so far as Life and joy are also endorsed, Equilibrium for that World's state and the Self will be easy to find. A strong Self, and strong Selves that are minimally Disturbed would be the best way to subjugate such a M.A.D.D.ness, and the power to do so comes from within.

Zero: In that case, wouldn't it be better universally for the authorities to be without a self? Motivations towards attaining higher power are intoxicating, and the capacity for self-disturbance would be ever present in an authoritative figure with a genuine self. The best authority would require maximum awareness of the world of concern while also discerning or assigning probability to possible motivations and disturbances in others without being motivated or disturbed.

One: That sounds an awful lot like Two, actually. Minus his acute motivations with us at all today, and his self-awareness.

Two: A Selfless version of me would only ever be in such a position of power if the responsibility was delegated to or entrusted to them. Or if some dire situation in the World of concern called for it. If the situation is good enough, or if the technology used Genuinely isn't sentient, then such individuals are rarely seen in any upper management or political spheres. But enough chit-chatting, I will tell you what an authority is, and then we will begin. An authority is a thing in power over itSelf or Others within a hierarchical system of concern.

Zero: That's… actually a pretty good definition for what we are using it for. In the more colloquial sense, it would be a thing in power over other things within a hierarchical system.

Two: Correct enough. Now One, make the first move. Command your subjects to take control of the board in this dark field.

One: Hmmm, let's see…in traditional chess, there are only 20 possible first moves. I can order each of my 8 pawns to move either one or two spaces forward, or my 2 knights two spaces forward and one space to the left or right. But this game won't be so simple, will it? Our pieces have selves and autonomous wills in play, and I need to consider that. Thus, they can and will be killed if I send them out to seize control. And to top it all off, our armies are at peace and in a solid, defensible position. Is it even ethical for me to make the first aggressive move? Is the initiation of war itself ever ethical?! Why cannot we all just cooperate, huh?

Two: War can be the ethical choice, even if it is rare and seldom done in the real World. Let's say that my army has already annihilated the nation of Three, and my being here implies that I plan to do the same to your nations and your people. Preventative injustices are typically not an ethical means for war. If a nation is driven by a sense of justice for the Three nation, the enemy is in a provocative stance, and they wish to prevent further injustices, then a declaration of war is ethical.

Zero: Then I would propose that it would be ethical for One and I to cooperate to bring your king to checkmate.

One: Our motivations and discernments of this chess world of concern are in alignment, Zero. Two's purple king must be brought to justice.

Two: Now let's suppose that Zero's nation desires to stay neutral during the whole ordeal, and let's suppose that One's nation tends to be racist and misogynistic and prejudiced against other nations, including Zero's. And I propose to Zero that I would not kill a single piece of his until One's king is in checkmate.

Zero: Naturally, it would be advantageous for me to secretly accept both of your proposals and let the two of you weaken each other while my pieces are relatively safe from harm. If I take One's deal only, my subject would be at peace, whilst destroying my objective pieces. But if I take Two's deal only, my subject would be disturbed, while either prolonging or avoiding harm entirely to my objective pieces.

One: If you even partially take Two's deal, then I will use the prejudice of my white pieces against your black pieces and start a race war against your spineless nation! Screw ethics, this is war, Zero! And Two's tyrant king must be stopped! And that end can justify many unjust means. So to ensure your cooperation, and to bring about the smallest number of casualties, grant me the power to move your pieces for you, Zero. Or even better, let's collaborate on every move so that we may move 2 times for every time Two moves.

Two: If you take One's deal, then I will exclusively attack your nation first. So to ensure your cooperation, I will lend you my troops to move as you please to end your race war as quickly as possible. After it is over, I will take over One's land and goods, and I will promise to leave your land in your hands in peace for the small yearly price of 6% of your total GDP. So what will it be?

Zero: Now it is impossible to stay neutral. If I side with One, I will be exclusively attacked and my power will be weakened, but I will have inner peace and no begrudging taxes without representation to pay. If I side with Two, I will be targeted, but not exclusively, and my power will increase, for we all know Two is the strongest among us. Plus, I don't think I could survive the onslaught of the exclusive wrath of an omniscient Two who would surely choose the best moves. So naturally, my best move would be to take Two's deal and collaborate by inquiring which moves would bring One's army into subjugation with the least amount of death to his pieces.

One: Unless I can provide Zero with an adequately motivational speech that appeals to taking down the purple king as an achievable challenge for long-term justice and tranquility, I'll be in checkmate before I even begin. So I would have to unconditionally forfeit my throne to survive.

Two: Then it would be just me versus Zero, 1 on 1. My king piece says our deal is Null and Void since the race war never began.

One: Thus, Two wins without a single piece ever being moved.

Zero: I kind of won as well, since nobody died. But at what cost? We were asked to take control of the board, and we chose to run away to save our skins. Our skins may yet be lost, for our lives now belong to a known killer. Surely, this is not the optimum scenario.

Two: Of course, force should be used against unambiguously Disturbed actors, if and when such a perfectly Aware system for Collective Equilibrium is put in a World. Of course, you two took my omniscience into account and your gamble to heel to my Disturbed purple king would likely save your skins at the cost of your freedom and your sense of justice. However, I shall inform you… no… *command* your black forces and white forces to work independently and cooperatively to stop my omniscient-backed and evil-acting purple force. Because if you work together, even when I make the perfect moves, I still can lose to the two of you. Also, One, your forces aren't racists and driven by prejudice any longer. Additionally, do not worry about the individual Selves amongst your forces. Grant them the Motivation and the Discernment to stop this evil power from spreading, and have them trust your judgment as well.

Zero: But my Lord! One and I still don't know what justice, good, and evil are. How can we be asked to move against an unambiguously evil actor while the term evil is still ambiguous? We brushed over it briefly when we defined discernment yesterday, but we never looked into what exactly these ethical judgments are. We also granted that the *accuracy* of the actions made had to be made to uphold a reasonable conversation, but the *ethicality* of the actions has not been granted to this degree.

One: Would you say, Zero, that even when an action is judged accurately, the same action can be judged as ethical *and* unethical, depending on whose self is discerning the action?

Zero: Not only that, but even identical actions in contrasting situations can change the verdict within the same self! Plus, I propose that we need to grant the ethicalness and unethicalness of an action to have a productive conversation about ethics.

One: Maybe not all actions. But if anyone wants to consistently know what actions are always ethical or always unethical, we would then have to grant the universal verdict attributed to these particular actions.

Zero: If you could posit such a set of actions, sure. So long as we agree that their ethicality or lack thereof isn't presupposed like what has to be granted concerning their perceptual accuracy, as in, the actions are genuine.

One: Of course. I guess that means I'm searching for objective moral claims that can be deduced to be universal regardless of who does it, where they do it, and when they do it.

Two: Yes, that is what this game is for! So please, start playing it! We can play while giving definitions of what the pieces are doing.

One: Then I propose, firstly, that in situations when and where an actor's actions done while in power are reasonably predefined to be evil, like in the case of Two's king, it is ethical to break certain traditional rules of war as a means to bring justice and peace. All is fair in love and war.

Zero: Wouldn't it be fair to make a synonymous comparison between something being *ethical* and something being *fair?* If something is fair, it is allowable and if it is allowable it follows the rules and regulations that would otherwise bar it from being allowed. It's not a perfect comparison though, because I think there are allowable things that are of non-ethical concern, for example, making answers that follow the laws of physics are themselves not ethical or unethical until the way those answers are used and relayed to others are considered.

Two: Not Everything allowable is fair, though. And not Everything ethical is allowable and fair. Sometimes the right thing to do requires breaking the rules. Sometimes the ethical thing to do is unfair to one or more parties involved.

One: So my first move that I believe is most reasonable would be to send my queen on a circular path either above or beside the board to assassinate Two's king from above or behind. But since only the knight has been known for genuinely going over other pieces' heads, she'll go beside and behind in a straight curved line, as if there were more playable spaces beyond the board.

Zero: Umm… I would argue that it is beyond the queen's capacity to move in an undefined and arbitrary curved line. If Two and I allow a hypothetical infinite expansion of a hexagonal 3-man chess board and consider those moves valid, I put your king in check with my queen from the start as well, and Two's queen puts me in check. Even if we are cooperating, you must mind the check from the first move.

Two: Incorrect. Only the *inner circles* between adjacent boards create a circular path of sorts, as you two described it. It is actually I who holds One in check, One holds Zero in check, and Zero holds me in check.

One: I see… In that case, I will move my queen behind my king so that both your king and queen are in check, so to speak.

Two: Even against an omniscient player, this 2 against 1 on an infinite board is absurdly impossible. Since our pawns have become all but useless, and seeing that our more powerful pieces can immediately go behind enemy lines without issue, my best move would be to move my left bishop behind my king. Zero would then send his right rook to kill my left rook, while One puts me in check again by sending his queen to kill my queen. My only reasonable option is to kill One's queen with my king. Zero sends his annoying rook to put me in check by killing my left knight, then One sends his left rook around to kill my right rook. Surely, you can see from here the power imbalances between our forces that I must face while being unable to do anything but deal with the checks you place in front of me. My king retreats immediately behind his right bishop, Zero finally moves his queen into action by killing my left bishop to put me in check, and then One moves his right rook back one placement to put it into action on the next turn. I move my right bishop between my king and Zero's queen, and Zero's queen moves back diagonally to the right 2 spaces from my perspective to put me in check again. Checks all around and inevitable! Even if mortal thinkers such as yourselves have no idea how to visualize such an onslaught and are unsure if what I say is Valid, then either take my word for it, watch a video that took this script and played it out, or draw it out yourself! Shoot, I'm just 4 moves away from checkmate, so I might as well finish it! One moves his right rook to the left 7 Spaces to put his second rook on the same circular trajectory as the first one was at the start. I move my right knight between Zero's queen and my king. Zero moves his queen forward to kill my knight to put me in check, and One moves his first rook into the same column as Zero's queen, and my evil king is in a Truly inevitable checkmate, never even needing his second rook. Only either of you acting like a joker or a fool instead of a knight could prevent it from happening, under the presupposed conditions of teamwork and an expanded hexagonal tiling of the board for us to play on. There are only a few dozen possible games to play, with very minor alterations, with the same inevitable conclusion of my demise for every one of them.

Zero: That's great and all, but what does that have to do with ethics?

Two: Nothing at all. I was just demonstrating that breaking some rules is more efficient at subjugating certain powers than Others. Plus, it seemed right to play out a game after all that build-up from yesterday.

One: But I have only moved one piece! Two, you did the rest of it all in your head!

Two: Why bring death to so many of our pieces, including all but 1 of my powerful forces, when there are better and more efficient outcomes to peace on the board by breaking a different rule? Since I am not evil, but the king of my people's forces is evil, in this case, it would be easier if I also cooperated with you guys to sabotage and assassinate my king.

Zero: So you could either break the rule that you cannot kill your own pieces, and use your own queen to kill your king, or you can move your king out into the open for us to easily kill him.

One: Hmmm… from this scenario, perhaps a few ethical concerns can be further inquired. Is breaking the rules in the name of justice a good decision to make? Does murder become acceptable when the murder victim did inherently evil things? And is it ethical for Two to throw the game and intentionally lose the sport?

Zero: That last question interests me. On one hand, games, competitions, and sports have rules to limit what moves are valid, but nothing is stopping a player from executing bad strategies within those limits. On the other hand, these things imply a will to victory motivating the player to play in the first place, and it could be argued that replacing the player's will to victory with a will to lose is unethical, in that it violates the spirit of the competition.

One: Yet even in sports where the capacities of different teams are nearly equal amongst themselves, the victory may be left to the team with the greater will to victory. Even within a self, this motivation towards victory can change depending on their circumstances in the world.

Two: What makes "throwing the game" of non-ethical or unethical concern depends on the gains made to the loser or losses to the winner within the World the games take place in. If there are no such objective gains or losses beyond the game, it is not an ethical concern how the player plays the game, because it is just a game. The subjective loss of the feeling of a well-earned victory being stolen by removing the well-earned part of the victory in an otherwise zero-sum game situation is a matter of social etiquette, not of ethics.

Zero: But Two, the game you propose to throw is surely not a zero-sum game situation! Our players have their selves on the line and to lose somebody in a battle should be devastating for any ethical authority in power, I propose.

One: Hmm… maybe. I think the only way to be sure is to thoroughly ask these two relevant questions. First, can an authority remain ethical while asking one of their subjects to commit an action that will lead to the subject's certain death? And secondly, to what extent is an authority liable to the actions of their subjects?

Zero: Interestingly, I think the answer to both of these questions is the same. If an authority gets their subject's reasonably informed consent beforehand, the authority would remain ethical. Likewise, suppose an authority is unaware or uninformed of the specific actions of their subjects. In that case, they shouldn't be held liable because they were never asked permission or gave their reasonably informed consent for them to commit the actions in question.

One: Ha! Zero! Did we stumble upon an objective moral guideline or law? Would I be speaking the truth if I said, "Thou shalt always ask for reasonably informed consent regarding actions that involve others?"

Zero: It is a fairly solid moral guideline to follow that stems from all 4 fundamental aspects of the self. But unfortunately no, it is not objective because it is not always the case. When a self is discovered to be a direct danger to itself or others and is disturbed beyond reason, then this guideline can be ethically disregarded.

One: Fair point, but I will not be dissuaded! Would I be speaking the truth if I instead said, "Thou shalt always *attempt* to receive reasonably informed consent before committing actions that involve others who are currently not a danger to themselves or others and have the functional capacity to reason?"

Zero: It may be true, but many words need to be clarified. What counts as an attempt? By whose discernment will we distinguish reasonable from unreasonable? What about consent that is given during the actions that involve themselves? What isn't dangerous under some other circumstance? And what makes a reason dysfunctional, clearly and objectively?

One: Half of those words were given by you first, Zero! Why am I being asked to define your words for you?

Zero: Hey, I'm not the one trying to codify those words into law. I was using them colloquially, while you were proposing to use them legally. Surely, you can see that the stakes for choosing wrong and ill-defined words are much higher for you than it is for me.

One: True. So it would be best for me to answer your questions one at a time, I suppose. And I would say that an attempt criterion would depend on the severity of the actions. A mundane action of typically small importance may only require a quick verbal exchange. An action, discerned significantly grand enough, may require a detailed written contract and an audio or video recording of the agreement to be considered a valid attempt.

Zero: So objective evidence of the consent makes an attempt valid?

One: Yes, and the more evidence you have, the better.

Zero: Fair enough. But there you said it again, *"an action discerned significantly grand enough."* BY WHOSE DISCERNMENT!?

One: The pre-validated authorities, of course. In the highest sense, by the authorities within the judicial system's discernment will reasonable attempts at receiving consent be judged. Typically, these judges appeal to the average discernment among the culture's population at the time, often referred to as *common sense.*

Zero: And what if those with uncommonly good sense discern that the common sense of their time is typically nonsensical, and the judges themselves operate with this common sense?

One: I think that question is out of bounds because it is a question of faith in the political power system which we agreed on presupposing. But not to leave you disappointed, the ideal government would naturally have those with uncommonly good discernment operating as judges in the first place, which would make your hypothetical highly unlikely to happen.

Zero: My mistake, I'll admit that. But cannot I still ask what is reasonable in-itself? And what is and is not logical?

One: Isn't reason simply discernments in action? If something isn't logical, doesn't it mean that the conclusion doesn't follow from the premises given?

Zero: Yes, but the thinker discerning the logic may not understand how the conclusion came to be from the premises given. What I'm saying is that the appearance of magic in the world mirrors incomplete logic and is often labeled as *magical thinking.* Then what distinguishes the logician's work that knows the conclusion, but disguises it from onlookers who then label the logician as a comedian once the trick has been revealed, from the truly incoherent madman? Could the logician be mistaken as a misunderstood maniac, and could the madman be mistaken for a well-intentioned comedian?

One: I suppose they could be mistaken for each other. Ultimately, the logician's reasoning can prove itself true under the ridiculous premises often supposed and can be replicated by asserting that the unlikely solution is correct. The madman can not distinguish premise from conclusion, nor repeat the process they took to reach their conclusion.

Zero: Hmm…that is fair enough, I reason. I propose the next question, then. What makes someone a sufficient danger to negate their right to consent on certain issues?

One: This question holds too many factors to answer with a single clear answer. Every primary aspect of the self holds a different factor, and different types of objects in the world are also factors. Unseen interactions and relations with others could also significantly change the probability of a harmful or otherwise problematic outcome.

Zero: I'm fine with multiple answers if they are clear and build up the bigger picture. So elaborate, if you will, these dangerous factors which concern others in the world.

One: Being in control of an object in the world that holds an appearance of potentially lethal harm to a living avatar of a self. Radioactive things, explosive things, flammable things, sharp things, poisonous things, and fast things come to mind.

Zero: I would add things that are really hot and really cold and things that could strangulate. And for my latter suggestion, if you would agree that they are dangerous things, clothes of all forms would be dangerous. Even arms and legs are potentially lethal to others, wherever a self uses them in a dangerous manner.

One: Like I said, it's only one factor. The presence of more factors increases the danger of the situation, or rather, the probability of a crime being committed nearby in the Mass-Electric-Space-Time of concern increases. A sharp object is almost always less dangerous than a fast and massive object, so clearly there is variance even within these factors. Different units to the different lethal objects within the danger dimension. One could even say the mass of the avatar containing the self correlates with the dangerousness of the avatar, but it should be a weak correlation due to the preponderance of other factors determining their dangerousness.

Zero: Such as…? In greater detail, I mean…

One: Having a high motivation towards power and control makes a self dangerous, regardless if they plan to use it for good or evil. Being highly disturbed mentally also makes somebody dangerous. Awareness and discernment in a self just change the type of dangerous self in question, from an evil genius, to a hopeless idiot, and from the chaotic in the thought only, to the clumsy in action. All selves hold the potential to be dangerous, save for the selfless. And like I said earlier, the active relations between a self and others tend to be more dangerous when they are close, and when communication and understanding between them are poor.

Zero: Does having great communication and understanding between selves make either self less dangerous? Couldn't one be deceiving the other, and thereby be even *more* dangerous whenever they lure the other into a false sense of relational security? I know that in this concept space, we have to assume the actions are genuine from the start, but in the real world, the active thoughts of the other would be considered in a self with adequate discernment.

One: Hmmm, I see your point. But I think such a possibility would lead such a discerning self towards inaction when dealing with the other. They would be more conservative and cautious towards what actions they perform. They would still wait for enough objective evidence in the world before interacting with the other. But given another's behavior and words appear genuine over a sizable period, I think the person who communicates can be labeled as safer than the random other you meet on the street.

Zero: What do you mean by sizable? Sounds like a quanta claim to me.

One: Hmmm… it is, but not a specific claim. I'm just saying greater amounts of time spent with another who appears to communicate and act genuinely should correlate with a lowered amount of danger attributed to them. There isn't an exact formula due to the many other factors involved here, even though this test of time appears to be the greatest predictor of reliability (and therefore safety) for pretty much everything in the world.

Zero: For what we are doing here, that is reasonable enough. Then again, things do break down over time, and again, an evil genius could…ah, never mind, it is reasonable enough, let it be so, myself! Now for the final question concerning your proposed objective moral statement. What shall be the verdict towards consent that was acquired during or after the action was committed? Does this delayed acceptance retroactively justify the crime? Or does the action have an indeterminate verdict until the other observes the consequences of the action, and discerns that they are either a victim or not?

One: I see now that the way I phrased the claim puts me in a double bind within the context of this question. If I double down on making it necessary to get consent before the action, then you would rightly point out that many would be guilty of victimless crimes, which is an absurd oxymoron that should be avoided in an ideal system of ethics. But if I allow for consent to be given after the fact of the action, then why would the layman bother asking before the action if they could coerce, manipulate, or otherwise convince the victim of their well-being later?

Zero: What's even worse still, is that by applying this law as it is, you criminalize the inaction of not getting consent, rather than criminalizing the actions themselves that create the deficit of victimhood in the first place.

One: Aye, yeah, yes, you're right! But surely it is still a good guideline for the individual to uphold to maintain lawful behavior, is it not?

Zero: Without a doubt, but this is not the objective law you were looking for. So what shall you do, One? Shall you refine your definition of consent once again? Will you dare propose that lawful behavior is always morally right? Or will you shift your attacks towards the actions that create the deficit of victimhood?

One: I believe the third option you provided is my best bet at a victory. And as if on cue, the sun begins to shine its light on me as we enter the crack of dawn of our early-morning battle on this third day. Also, there would be no point in tackling lawful behavior being always morally right until I have successfully submitted something that is objectively lawful.

Zero: Precisely. So, I assume you will attempt to define murder as a crime.

One: If there was hope to find a crime where there was always a victim, it would be either pre-meditated murder or rape, I think.

Zero: My friend, how would you define this objectively criminal action?

One: Murder is the objectively harmful disturbance of another's avatar that removes their self from the world of concern.

Zero: Within the bounds of that definition, aren't we murderers every Now we go and hunt a wild beast that attacked our ranks during a campaign? Shall Two lock us up for defending him from a lion, a bear, or a hog that has demonstrated its hostility?

One: Of course not, that would be absurd! Surely I meant the disturbance of another's avatar *of the same species.*

Zero: By that better definition, wouldn't the selves within our chess pieces be considered guilty of murdering Two's king?

One: I wouldn't think so, but that does raise a good point concerning the concept of war. I believe that every self who enters the battlefield as a soldier gives their consent to be fought against to the point of death.

Zero: Hmmm, I can see that being reasonable. Then in the same line of reasoning, the wild beasts also create a battlefield of sorts whenever they attack us, thereby justifying our act of killing them. So would you say that every instigator consents to be killed? Also, what if they are coerced into fighting in the first place and do not understand the full concepts behind the instigation?

One: Yes, I believe every armed and dangerous instigator consents to be killed. And even if they are coerced, that doesn't make them any less dangerous in the Now. In this instance, we can still note that killing an armed and dangerous instigator of an attack is not murder, but self-defense.

Zero: Then I suppose that when a child maliciously and unrelentingly kicks you in the shins with steel-toed boots, it is perfectly valid to kill them.

One: I… um… I guess it does depend on the force of the attack, doesn't it? A hefty kid kicking you with steel-toed boots relentlessly could prove lethal by bleeding out, couldn't it? But a toddler in sneakers isn't a sufficient threat to justify killing them.

Zero: If it depends on the force of the initial attack that justifies the killing, would it not also depend on the capacity of the avatar of a victim to withstand the attack?

One: Kind of. I suppose giving the adult victim shin guards would somehow make his killing of the hefty kid less justifiable, wouldn't it?

Zero: What's even worse still, is that investigators would consider the child a murder victim, rather than a casualty of self-defense, if the adult ever discerns that his life is in danger.

One: If I am to have any chance of making an objective law, I should define two equally capable civilian adults such as ourselves, where one attacks the other in an objectively vulnerable state with deadly force when the victim did nothing to instigate an attack.

Zero: And at that point, you wouldn't be defining murder anymore, but merely *describing a specific murder.* It would be a representative case law, describing a scenario in the world that is a thing you have yet to adequately define in-itself. We had no problem defining things in the world two days ago. Mass will always be as we defined it, so long as it persists. Space will always be as we defined it, so long as it persists. Since words are representations of things and actions, surely you are capable of defining murder in a way where it will always be as you define it.

One: Remember when we were defining running, and we agreed that running was the totality of situations where the action defined took place? As an action, murder is the same way.

Zero: I understand that. But as yet, you seem to have defined walking as running by calling this act that was clearly self-defense *murder.* And I predict that if you were to go on, you would distinguish killing in self-defense from murder by suggesting that the death caused in self-defense is either ethical or non-ethical, and that murder is unethical.

One: It is this way, isn't it!?

Zero: Not objectively and absolutely, no. I give you a counter-example to both. Killing in self-defense against an attacker who is using non-lethal use of force is unethical. And surely you wouldn't fault any of our chess pieces if they had the means to murder the evil purple king in his sleep. They would be labeled an ethical hero, wouldn't they?

One: They might. Or they might be labeled an unethical assassin. I guess it depends if Two's army raises another king to win the war or not, and who writes the history of the event.

Zero: Don't make me laugh, One! Surely, you didn't suggest that the judgment for the ethicality of the murder of the purple king will be left in the hands of the victor of the war? You cannot in the same breath say that murder is inherently unethical, and leave the judgment of the actions' ethicality in the hands of the particular set of others who are left to judge it!

One: You trapped me! The reason such a murder could be pardoned in the first place is because it is the far lesser of two evils! One life for an entire nation's worth of victims is an ethical tradeoff in lieu of more nations becoming victimized in the future.

Zero: So the punishment fits the crime, in essence.

One: Precisely.

Zero: Then please don't dawdle, One. Is there any way you can define the crime of murder in such a way that it will always be ethically wrong?

One: In a world where there are no bad or evil actors, I probably could. In a world passionately avoiding torture, harm, and hate, I probably could. If I add those caveats to the definition, it may hold up, so let me try again. Is murder the objectively harmful disturbance of another's body (when they have not assaulted anybody with lethal force with intent) that results in the removal of the other's self from the world of concern?

Zero: That's pretty good, actually. It could be worded better, though. But wouldn't you agree that perpetuated assault with non-lethal force, in other words, torture would be a sufficient caveat to put in as well?

One: No, actually. It would make the definition unclear again, since we can see that there is a blurred line between annoyance to torture. I now agree with your perspective, that it is subjective to the duration and the prerequisite forces of an assailant, and even other consequences of the situation that could be determined to range from justifiable self-defense to manslaughter to homicide to senseless murder. So although I agree that torture *could* justify the killing of another, because it is not always the case, I chose to leave it out.

Zero: That definition covers what murder is to the highest range that reason alone can deduce, without spilling over into different but similar ideas. We can say that in most cases, murder is the intentional objective disturbance of another of the same species (who themselves haven't acted with lethal intent) that results in the complete removal of their self from the world of concern.

One: It's so odd, Zero. My defeat today so far is certain, yet I feel obliged to review why I'm losing so that I may win later. Murder is indeed how you just defined it, regardless of an appeal to any law given. And no matter the situation, a more harmful or more evil scenario could be forced upon a self to ethically justify acting upon the lesser of two or more evils. Not to mention…

Zero: Woah there, Sparky. I agree with what you said, but we have not gotten there yet. We have only defined murder in such a way that doesn't rely on its unethical or unlawful attribute to be what it is. It's a whole other thing to say that all lesser evil actions are justified when faced with a certain and greater evil.

One: Is it not obvious?

Zero: Not inherently, no it is not. Maybe provide a clear scenario that demonstrates the truth of the proposition.

One: Fine, then. Let's imagine that the evil purple king is less like an Adolf Hitler-type character, and more like a Jigsaw-type character from the thriller series *Saw*. He puts you in a heavily guarded glass box with an innocent 4-year-old girl strapped to a guillotine with a lever inside the glass box with you. Outside this glass box are 100 relatively free children who you can see are contained within a larger white room with cameras, speakers, & gun turrets positioned on the ceiling and walls. The purple king speaks his will from the speakers, "You are here because you believe in objective morality. I will make a murderer out of you today. You have 4 options. You can pull the lever, which will certainly kill the 4-year-old in the box with you. If you do this, you and the other kids will walk out of here completely free and alive. Or you can choose not to pull the lever, which will prolong everyone's captivity, plus I will order my pawns to kill one of the other 100 kids for every hour you choose not to pull the lever. If you succeed in not pulling the lever for 100 hours, you and the 4-year-old girl will walk out of here completely free and alive. Or you can step out of the box right now, which will result in my pawns randomly killing half of the children who remain, then you and the other half of the children will walk out of here completely free and alive. Or you can choose to switch places with the

4-year-old girl to commit suicide, then we will pull the lever for her, but doing so will come with the sacrifice of 10 of the relatively free children, so if you choose this option in the first hour. 91 others will walk out of here completely free and alive. If any of the other 100 kids try to leave, they alone will be killed." After two hours of verifying the situation, you will have seen two kids be shot on the hour. Another kid was shot for trying to leave, forcing you to come to terms with the reality of the situation, where the more inactive you are in the situation, the more unethical and unjust death will occur. Only one more, typically unethical and unjust, death directly caused by your own actions will cease this horrible situation. This causes murder to be the most ethical thing to do in this conceptual world of concern.

Zero: Almost perfect, One. Who in their right mind would select the completely inactive action?

One: If the 4-year-old was a precious loved one, and the others were unknown foreign children, it would make the option appealing.

Zero: Would the inactive option be murder, though? Wouldn't the purple king and his minion pawns be the true murderers in this case? I'm not sure if coercion of this degree would be considered murder.

One: I suppose you're right, but it would still be the self's murder that would optimally end the situation, based on the definition you gave.

Zero: Shoot, you're right. Murder is the intentional *and direct causation of* the objective disturbance of another…yada yada, the rest is fine.

One: Absolutely. Do you still agree that the actual murder committed by the self is still the most ethical option of the 4?

Zero: No doubt. But why is that the case?

One: Perhaps it's simply the actions that maximize human life and well-being given the circumstances?

Zero: It stands to reason for that to be the case, yes.

One: Then tell me, Zero, how is this not the objective base for all morality that I was looking for in the first place?

Zero: You said it yourself, *"and."* Sometimes the actions that maximize human life minimize well-being. And sometimes the actions that maximize well-being minimize human life.

One: I offer another jab at winning, for the sport of it. What if it is only the maximizing of human life that is the objective moral claim that underlies all ethics? What if well-being is simply an extension of human life?

Zero: Even then, sometimes the viability of different human lives are at odds against one another. In your horrific Jigsaw scenario, we can still ask, "Whose life are we seeking to maximize?" The self? Others they love? The total quanta?

One: It must be the last one! The totality of ethically acting humans who reinforce the collective society.

Zero: If it is, I offer one final rebuttal to ensure the continuation of my victory on this third and final day. Let's suppose the purple Jigsaw king offers one final option, a 5th option, for you to choose from. He says to you, "Or you can torture this girl every hour for the next 14 years. Everyone but her will be adequately fed, educated, and entertained to distract them from the atrocities you will be committing. We'll switch out the glass box for a soundproof room to not scar the other children, replace the guillotine with a bondage stretcher, and we won't kill any of the other children for simply trying to leave. Every day, you will be required to perform each of the following: remove a fingernail or toenail, provide at least a single 2nd-degree burn, bring her body temperature to below 95° Fahrenheit, cut her to produce at least 8 ounces of blood, sexually penetrate her with an unpleasant object of your choosing, and she must never leave a malnutritious state starting a month from now. After 14 years of captivity, you will all leave completely free and alive, and only the girl and perhaps yourself will be the only ones psychologically scarred during your lengthy stay." Now, One, if it is *only* the total quantity of ethically acting human lives you are concerned with, the most objectively ethical thing to do would be the 5th option, because that is what the situation calls for, and you will surely return to an ethical way of being at the end of it, won't you? You aren't the monster in this situation, it is the purple Jigsaw king who is the real monster.

One: Zero, you sadistic thinker! I concede completely, for clearly it would be better to just kill the poor girl than to force her, and you, for that matter, to endure those activities during the formative years of her life! Especially if that evil purple king made the 5th option indefinite rather than a determinate 14 years, it would be better to kill her!

Zero: Thus, even though well-being is an extension of human life, we just deduced that it is conceivable that a significant depreciation of well-being can make death the ethically superior option. Therefore, the ethicality of an action depends on the quantity of life forms *and* the quality of life affected as a result of the action, and to a lesser degree, how the action is perceived by those who are affected by the actions.

One: Is that all? I'm curious, because in the world, there are 4 primary dimensions, and in the self, there are 4 core attributes. It seems oddly incomplete for the society of others to have only 3 fundamental factors underlying all ethics.

Zero: Hey, I'm all ears for any suggestions. Let's use our antsy pawns to see if they can help uncover anything they could unethically do to each other. My pawn will play the victim, Two's will be the criminal, and One's will be both defender and investigator of justice. Now One, can you think of an unethical act where the qualia or quanta of life of the victim wasn't disturbed, and the victim is unaware of the crime, yet there is still a crime to be observed?

One: I've got a few ideas. Some cases of theft. Maybe taxation, when the money doesn't go where the taxed want it to go. Graffiti to the house of a blind man. Some cases of false marketing. I think these have an objective depreciation of capital value, and imply the other's capacity to be in passive possession of other things.

Zero: I'm inclined to disagree. Aren't these examples of an indirect loss to the victim's quality of life, as in a loss of net capital reduces the victim's total capacity to buy things that could increase the duration of their life or increase their life's well-being?

One: Shoot, I guess that's right. Hmmm, but what if the purple pawn has *the victim* as a possession? Like a parent, legal guardian, or some other dependent relationship. If the criminal is inactive and neglectful concerning the victim, wouldn't that produce a new factor to ethics?

Zero: Not at all, actually. By neglecting a dependent, they criminally reduce their dependent's quality of life; a form of torture, I'm sure you'll agree. If you think about it, neglect is another example of an indirect loss to the victim's quality of life.

One: Then the intent of the perpetrator doesn't count as a factor? I'm confused.

Zero: The criminal's intent only adds to the intensity and degree to which the other factors add to the crime.

One: With that logic, it follows that there are only 2 fundamental factors underlying all ethics. Because the absolute loss of life, as described by the reduction in the quantity of life, is the maximum loss to the victim's quality of life.

Zero: Look at you, doing my job for me, a solid observation!

One: Further still, the 2 remaining factors can again be condensed to be viewed as 1 again. Whether the victim or the judge observes or feels the effects of the crime, life in some form will be reduced. It may be best to keep the fundamental factors underlying ethics as 2, but reworded as the reduction of livelihood in the world, and the reduction of livelihood in the self. Only the first is required to commit a valid crime, but it is the sympathy and empathy of seeing the reduction of livelihood in others that underlies all ethical evaluations.

Zero: Is it, though? Would you discern that a healthy man going on a fast is unethical? There would be a clear loss of livelihood after a few days, correct?

One: In that particular case, the livelihood of the self is especially important! The self could grow in esteem and become more disciplined, which would certainly increase the self's livelihood!

Zero: But what if it doesn't? Is it unethical to motivate others to go on a fast by making it a religious obligation to do so?

One: I mean…it is certainly debatable. The intensity of this kind of peer pressure can vary between different situations, so to answer your question, it depends. When a self is motivated towards self-discipline, it is ethical, but when fasting is used as a tool for disciplining others to engage in fasting behavior, it is unethical.

Zero: Good answer.

One: So the reduction of livelihood, and the full analysis thereof, taking all involved selves into account, is still my proposal for what underlies ethical judgments.

Zero: It's a good proposal, and you used it well. But let's make it a great proposal. So tell me, then, what is livelihood?

One: Is it not everything we have discussed today so far? Is it the appearance of having secured the qualities of life?

Zero: Vaguely. More like possessing life's necessities.

One: I see… Well, what are life's necessities?

Zero: It depends on the life form.

One: True… But is there anything that all life forms need to remain alive?

Zero: It depends on what you mean by "life."

One: Must we continue digging for more fundamental bases? Ethics is based on livelihood, and livelihood is based on life, and life is based on existence, which is based on its energy in the world of concern.

Zero: Exactly. And so, we don't need to dig any further, because we already discussed those more fundamental layers. The better question to focus on would be to understand what life is, so we can understand livelihood, so we can finally understand the most accurate moral structure to teach others in the future.

Two: We know what Life means. I told you last week, remember?

Zero: Aye, this is true, but we, and by we, I mean One and I, do not yet know if any of those meanings of life apply to all forms of life, and are mutually exclusive to life. We know life holds the capacity to fulfill its meaning, but we don't yet know if non-life can also fulfill the meanings of life. We wouldn't want to make the mistake of declaring something that was never alive "life" just because it holds something in common with life.

One: Two, may you please remind us of the meanings of life?

Two: Life is what I, your Leader, say it is. It is the experience of itSelf. It is Productive. It seeks out beauty. It reacts to fearful stimuli. It increases in Self-Awareness. It learns and seeks the Truth. It's ultimately meaningless. But it exists, even though its status as Life in-itself is indeterminate. It increases entropy. It minimizes Disturbance and maximizes Equilibrium to find peace. It seeks the successful reProduction of its cells or traits. Its meaning is subjective. Life is adaptable. It experiences pain and pleasure. It holds the capacity to love. It seeks acceptance from the Others. It acknowledges the culture of the Collective. It holds the capacity for growth. Life will inevitably die. It is its literal definition. Lastly, Life tends to create Order. That is all.

Zero: There are a lot of redundancies.

Two: I consider it to be thorough. I made sure it covers Everything, since it is its subjective definition, the possibility of its definition being in error is almost guaranteed.

One: But doesn't that imply that things and actions not caused by life nor conducive to life can erroneously provide life with meaning?

Two: Correct.

One: Then isn't this our duty to fully distinguish life from non-life, so that livelihood and truly right and ethical living can be known in full?

Two: *Your* duty, sure, but not mine. I've already foreseen what happens when I do and when I don't perform this duty, and Nothing ultimately changes. Ironically, you two doing this provides just as much short-term change as if I just delegated it to you, so why waste my Energy if you can figure it out for yourSelves?

Zero: So you won't feel bad if we rip the definition down to its most fundamental bones?

Two: Sometimes you don't listen very well, Zero. I already know the fundamental bones, and I just delegated you the optional duty to find them. Why would I be mad or sad? Just because I added skin and muscles to the first definition, doesn't make it wrong or incomplete if you clarify the bones supporting the whole structure.

Zero: Alrighty then! I just haven't had the pleasure of negating your words yet, Two. Firstly, many times over, you said, "The meaning of Life is its own Qualitative description." Sure, the *meaning of life* requires words, but does *life in-itself* require words?

One: Not in-itself, but the presence of words could be used as evidence that the thing in question is alive and aware.

Zero: It doesn't exactly do a good job at distinguishing life from non-life, either. Books hold words, but they aren't alive. Computer programs can be made to create words artificially, too. Accidental or entropy-caused sequences can stumble upon the creation of word-like things all the time. I'm sure the words A and I come up a lot in nature.

One: True, but can the comprehension of the words be reproduced in non-life?

Zero: No, but can the lack of comprehension of the words be used as evidence of the presence of non-life within the thing in question?

One: Well…yeah, actually. There may be a lot of false positives of life not comprehending the words. But without a doubt, 100% of non-life will lack the comprehension of meaningful stimuli.

Zero: Good point. So life can comprehend meaningful stimuli, huh?

One: It sounds a little bit like discernment in the self.
Zero: That's what I was thinking. How else could a stimulus mean something to the living thing unless it could be discerned and distinguished from a lack of stimulus?
One: Maybe it could misfire towards false comprehensions, but it certainly has this capacity to fire in the first place!
Zero: But we mustn't get too far ahead of ourselves! Remember, it is the comprehension of the self's discernment that denotes life, not the words themselves. It is the sensory response that demonstrates the thing's capacity to learn, that demonstrates its life.
One: Let's call it… comprehension. Life can comprehend the world and itself in some capacity. What else can you comprehend about life in-itself, Zero?
Zero: Two was redundant on another point, I think. In essence, he said, "Life is active" several times over.
Two: Incorrect. The specific actions are distinct and important. Even Comprehension can be reworded to mean "active thought." Non-Life can also be active, as Time decrees that an object in motion tends to stay in motion unless another Force acts upon it; whether that Force is Living or not does not matter. Try again.
Zero: I see… then how about the phenomenon of productivity? You said that life is both productive *and* reproductive. So isn't reproduction just production with an extra step?
Two: Much better. One, please continue this investigation.
One: The meaning of production is to maintain a self's livelihood, isn't it? Reproduction also maintains some aspects of a self and passes this duty onto a similar other.
Zero: Is being productive a duty?

One: To remain alive, yes. Life becomes non-life if it doesn't maintain itself or is unable to maintain itself. Life is obligated to remain what it is for as long as possible, for if it didn't, it would already be demonstrating the characteristics of what it is not.

Zero: An astute observation. But what about the opposite extreme of being productive, as in being *over-productive,* if they also began demonstrating characteristics of non-life?

One: It depends on the situation. It may be a form of self-sacrifice to maintain a greater livelihood in the others, a self, or a significant other reproduced. Or the self's livelihood may be so deprived that it must do this in seeking out its equilibrium, even if that equilibrium is unachievable.

Zero: So it isn't to say, "The more productive life is, the better," but rather "The minimal level of effort required to maintain the livelihood of the self and others you are responsible for is the right amount of productivity?"

One: Kind of. If the self in question is strong, more effort can increase the livelihood of the others the self concerns themselves with, without overexerting themselves. And as for the weak who cannot even maintain themselves, their salvation to continue in life will come from either these strong others or luck. But what I'm trying to say is, for most people, all efforts between minimal and a *mindfully efficient* maximum are conducive to life.

Zero: No offense, but that's not saying much. It's almost a tautology to say, "To be productive is to put forth the effort!"

One: As you put it, sure, but is it a tautology to say, "Life is productive, and life does this by putting forth effort towards itself and other life forms?"

Zero: I guess not… but riddle me this, One. Can non-life also be productive towards itself and other non-life forms?

One: I suppose both gravitational and electromagnetic forces could be viewed this way. But I was referring to a kind of *motivational effort* towards the self and others.

Zero: In that case, it appears correct. So far, life has just been different aspects of the self in action. To continue the trend, what would disturbance in action look like, One?

One: I'd be afraid to find out. But I imagine it would be the dissipation of a life form barrier in some form.

Zero: That covers life definitionally increasing entropy and its inevitable death. And a couple of other points to lesser degrees. Entropy as consumption is probably a notable kind of dissipation as well.

One: Productivity requires energy. The capacity to acquire this energy and convert it into useful energy for productive work can vary depending on the energy source and the life form. It is this conversion process we are investigating.

Zero: But wait, couldn't we create non-living things to do the energy-converting process for us?

One: Hmmm… I suppose?

Zero: And in general, everything in the world has its overall entropy increasing with time, which includes life, and non-life alike. So everything but the Energy of the world in-itself is dissipating.

One: So it's not specific enough, huh?

Zero: It's on par with saying, "Life is Energy." It does little to nothing to distinguish what it is from what it is not.

One: Then let's ask another question. Is there a specific kind of dissipation unique to life that can distinguish it from non-life? The first things that come to my mind are consumption, excreta, love, and war. Possibly inhaling and exhaling too, but that may be a kind of consumption and excreta. Maybe organism growth and death too.

Zero: Hmmm… The love and war dichotomy may be valid. The other 3 dichotomies you mentioned appear to be functions of utility toward life. For example, as a kind of proto-life form, stars consume and excrete themselves and random interstellar objects. The sun's excrement, as simple electromagnetic radiation, becomes the useful energy of consumption for plants, and so on the cycle of life continues. The birth, consumption, and inhaling of a star is driven by mass phenomena such as gravity, and it excretes and exhales relatively pure electric phenomena as light, and the death of the star dissipates these fundamental building blocks of matter out into the real world.

One: The way I see it, I have two or three choices. I can ignore your input entirely, but let's face it, that is more of a non-option. Or I can posit that everything is alive based on the evidence of it dissipating to promote panpsychism. Or I have to admit that these kinds of dissipation as described don't define life, but something more fundamental.

Zero: Or you could redefine life's consumption as specifically the use of adenosine triphosphate (ATP) at the cellular level as the particular energy of choice used to fuel itself.

One: … Wow. Thanks for the help. So wait, does this mean viruses count as life?

Zero: If One were to accept that definition as given, yes. But if One would rather tweak the definition and clarify that only cells that can produce adenosine triphosphate *on their own* count as life, then no, viruses wouldn't count as life.

One: So viruses require another to animate themselves?! Parasitic and weak, they are! Living non-life, ambiguously standing between life and non-life! I choose this second definition, these harbingers of death have no place being classified as life!

Zero: Yet you would gladly embrace the potent and deadly bacteria and the truly alive parasites as life. Being a cell and using ATP as its energy is good enough for me. I pick the first definition. Besides, these definitions don't include robotic and artificial life forms that don't use ATP but can to an ambiguous degree demonstrate a self. And if we continue to grant the assumption that their actions and behaviors are genuine just like everybody else, life's definition would need to expand even further to include abiotic life also.

One: Good… Well, in that case, how could abiotic life ever exist? If biology as the study of life itself is lacking life to study by being abiotic, how would you suggest somebody observe life where it is lacking?

Zero: It's not a contradictory oxymoron, I assure you. Although abiotic life would lack this cellular consumption of ATP, it may still comprehend the world and itself, and be productive towards its means.

One: Would it be safe to say that life lacking the capacity for one of these fundamental aspects of life only makes it less life-like, but doesn't negate its life in full?

Zero: I would think so. If it holds all of life's fundamental aspects, it is definitely life. If it holds none of them, it is certainly non-life. But if it only holds some of them, it is either ambiguous or some kind of lesser form of life. The bio-part of biology generally refers to requiring the investigation of something that certainly has the cellular consumption of ATP in the life of concern because that observation is objective in the world. Comprehension is subjective, and being productive also holds some subjectivity with it.

One: That makes sense. So I ask, are there any more objective components to life that can be used to distinguish it from non-life, so we can know how to study abiotic life when the time comes?

Zero: Not pure objective, but perhaps a blend where the objective component refers to the environment the life form lives in. Like, life lives in a suitable environment. Non-life does not have this restriction, by the looks of it. But what counts as "suitable" is subjective to the life form. Although I can imagine a nuclear-powered abiotic life form whose environment could almost match that of non-life, even if they find traversing to the inside of a black hole a bit problematic to sustain their life.

One: Ha, we may be faced with another absurdity in addition to what we experienced two days ago. Remember how observing any individual part of energy implied the whole of Energy? Zero, is it true that observing the individual life form implies the life of the whole ecosystem?

Zero: Hmmm… Typically, this is the case, but not always. Living cells don't imply a living human, and an astronaut observed on the moon doesn't imply the viability of the moon's ecosystem. The reverse should also make this clear, when observing a living human does not imply that the individual cell that comprises the human is necessarily alive. Also, a living ecosystem does not imply the life of the forms within it, since the dead don't suddenly leave the ecosystem after dying. So, can life be defined by its preferred habitat?

One: Not if it is adaptable enough to be observed in a habitat of significant contrast to their preferences.

Zero: That's why I think life is adaptable. But the more adaptable the life form is, the less useful it is to define the life form by the environment it is observed in.

One: The range of variables in the environment being used to test the life form's capacity to adapt… This can still be done for abiotic life forms as well.

Zero: Can this range be tested? Even in the same species, different members can have different ranges. If the life forms are tested to go beyond that range, they would die, which would arguably be unethical and meaningless, since it would apply only to the individual. A large sample of the population would need to be killed to calculate this true range. And this range can drift over time in as little as a few generations, making the information non-applicable once again.

One: Zero, humans do this to bacteria already, and some quickly reproducing insects. Surely, you wouldn't consider using antibacterial soap unethical to the poor, defenseless bacteria living life on your hands, would you?

Zero: To mankind, of course not. Especially towards harmful bacteria. But if a bacterium could produce the actions of such an experiment on the other bacteria, and comprehend the results of those actions, then it would be unethical for the bacteria to do so.

One: Zero, you are an odd fellow. And you make an odd point that I think I agree with. This makes me think of an odd tangent to follow. Let's say we are right. What is unethical to the bacteria is ethical for humans. What would your verdict be if an insect could produce the test on the bacteria and comprehend the results? Would it be ethical or unethical to genocide the bacteria races?

Zero: I discern that the insect would have a higher moral obligation to distinguish which particular bacteria races to exterminate. Or perhaps not a moral obligation, but a utilitarian obligation. Why kill a lesser other if they could only ever benefit themselves? And why allow a lesser other to maintain their life if they could only ever put the life of themselves in jeopardy?

One: Your first question is obvious. Another being beneficial and harmless would be senseless to kill. But your second question isn't so clear. I can think of a good reason to let them live. Being harmful doesn't negate these lesser other's capacity to be beneficial for the self. In fact, being harmful could prove itself to be very beneficial when controlled like a tool in the right skillful hands. To exterminate harmful others more proves a lack of creativity towards greater productivity in the self. Either that or a lack of care.

Zero: Interesting… I don't disagree. So would you say the evil purple king chose to do evil simply because he lacked the creativity and care necessary to incorporate the other nation's people to enhance his productivity *peacefully?*

One: It's a theory, anyway. But yes, I would say that.

Two: A correct theory! Plus, Zero, in addition to what One pointed out, the 2nd question you posed can be reworded to make your moral proposition clear again for the insect. Why allow any Other to maintain *their freedom* if they could only put the Life of the Self in jeopardy?

Zero: Yes, thank you, I see… Not all kinds of dissipation are dangerous. But when it is dangerous, having the capacity to keep it in order becomes more vital the more dangerous it is. Like keeping a shorter leash on a pit bull dog, locks on a gun cabinet, or thick layers surrounding nuclear radiation containers.

One: Agreed. But to answer your reformed question, there are others, and frankly, myself as well, who would rather give up their life rather than lose their freedom, precisely because they comprehend that their capacity to grow and produce will be handicapped, thus handicapping life for themselves. I say the objective danger of the thing or other in question should be what dictates the level of control imposed on the thing or other.

Zero: For things, yes, but for others, it should be the harm caused by their actions. The objective depreciation of life, I mean.

Two: My loyal subjects, you have the correct deductions on ethics. Very close to correct, indeed. But my friends, there is another Fundamental Aspect of Life that you missed. There are Four here as well. I'll give you a hint: it has to do with the freedom to go where it can, and the love, acceptance, and acknowledgment of the Other.

One: Validation, perhaps? Validation of its fitness to be life?

Zero: Really, Two? Survival of the fittest, in the form of mercy, given by more powerful others? Don't make me laugh!

Two: Not mercy, but a judgment. One was more correct, and you merely mentioned its most famous application. Life endures the tests and challenges it faces within itSelf and in the World. Although the failure of all Life is inevitable, its salvation comes from the mercy, love, and care of the Other. While there is Life, complete control and subjugation will not work for longer than a few generations, and cooperation and cohabitation are the most successful methods for Life with the Other by a large margin. Nobody can be the strongest or most fit for every trial Life forms may face, And when the trials of Life are too much, if Nobody saves you, you will surely transition into Non-Life rapidly. The freedom to go your own way and face these trials, and the love, mercy, and acceptance of Others who reciprocate this form of Validation no matter the outcome, is the Way towards even greater Life forms.

Zero: Wow… I shall not dare refute this truth. I don't think it is possible. I think in the span of a single lifetime, an individual could successfully conquer and subjugate all others, but unless the system successfully selects its most powerful and capable into this system of subjugation, it wouldn't last long. Too much overturn of power is unstable, and maintaining such power unchecked for long and indefinite periods becomes unstable for those who wield this power.

Two: Precisely. And when the Other rejects you, whether in hatred, judgment, or whenever their own trials overwhelm them, Validate them regardless, and try to Comprehend them so that if they begin their assault, you can be victorious with the superior powers of love and wisdom. These powers will overwhelm the hatred of fools.

One: I suppose validation does seek out homeostasis, as a sort of peace with others in the world, huh?

Two: Not just with Others, but with the Self as well. It checks up on itSelf to ensure that Life is near Equilibrium. It responds adequately when Life is not as it should be, for inadequate responses to Disequilibrium lead to the path of Non-Life swiftly.

One: So life includes some combination of these 4 things. Comprehension is the ability to learn and distinguish the self from others and things in the world. Production is the ability to maintain a viable livelihood for itself and/or others. ATP consumption is the ability to use adenosine triphosphate as its primary source of energy. And validation is the ability to endure disturbances in the world and keep them minimal to confirm the life of the self from the perspective of others.

Zero: Meh, it's good enough. It's getting close to lunchtime already, and I could go for a nap as well. We didn't come here to discuss life, we came here to determine the ideal ethical structure to interact with others. So, One, if this is indeed what life is, how would you propose livelihood to be defined as a function of life?

One: Isn't it obvious? Whatever promotes comprehension, production, ATP consumption, and validation of the other promotes the livelihood of the other. And whatever demotes these things in the other demotes their livelihood as well.

Zero: Ha, I guess it is obvious, huh? Then here is my final proposition. I say that although it is generally the case that promoting the livelihood of the self and the other is an ethical truth we can live by, and demoting livelihood is usually unethical, it is still not always the case in either set of circumstances.

One: In isolation, yes, you're right. You've already convinced me with the plethora of examples you've already given. Surely, promoting the comprehension and production of weapons of grand destruction is probably unethical. Promoting the ATP consumption of cancer cells in others is probably unethical. Validating the actions of the evil purple king in-themselves is probably unethical. But maybe, just maybe, the negation of all 4 of the fundamental aspects of life could offer us the basis for laws to tell us what not to do.

Zero: Hmmm… That's an interesting proposition. So you're saying that if an action reduces all 4 aspects of life, it becomes an objective moral claim?

One: I think so, yes. I think if there was any chance to make objective morality a valid philosophical proposition, this would be the way to do it. One would have to confirm life as the objective basis for the good of morality, even as an ontological necessity. Then One would simply have to reasonably demonstrate that the immoral action would lower the subjective aspects of comprehension, productivity, and validation.

Zero: I agree, this is what One would have to do. Maybe not the precise words, but I understand what you mean. But I disagree that there is any chance to be had. Just look at Two again! His comprehension has maxed out, and yet his productivity towards life in his kingdom is Zilch! Even when we consider everybody's comprehension, we can see time and time again that increasing comprehension too much in certain fields can decrease overall productivity. *It makes them lost in thought!*

Two: One, I cannot be the standards for Validation and Comprehension concerning the ethicality of your actions. If a Living subject becomes the standard, then your Self's Validation and Comprehension amount to Nothing. Sacrificing the Self's Life for my sake adds Nothing to my Comprehension of you, so don't do it. Be more like me, by being your own best standard.

One: But my Lord, I cannot validly validate myself! If I did, then I could discern to do whatever I was motivated to do!

Zero: No friend, think! Valid validation can and should be validated by the other. If the other invalidates your actions, then this is evidence that there is a lack of comprehension somewhere, and those with discernment would seek it, even if it is in themselves, so that adequate corrective actions can take place. It's also possible the other simply lacked the comprehension of the situation in the world the action-in-question took place in.

Two: Remember One, I persist in the concept Space in your Self at all Times. And you know that not Everything in concept Space applies to real Space. So can my Validations towards you be invalid in the real World?

One: I guess… some day, they would *have* to become invalid…

Two: Doesn't this form of invalidation apply to all Others as well? Isn't what you perceive in the Other not as they are, but an erred approximation of what their genuine Motivations, Awareness', Discernments, and Disturbances are?

One: Of course! Imperfect perceptions are inevitable!

Two: Then hear the words of Two! No matter which Self or Others you put your trust in the correct arbitration of moral values, it is always your Discernment and Validations of these values that give the ethical statutes power! Moral actions and immoral actions alike require the subjective Self to Discern that the invalidation of a particular Life is one or the other. Observe and realize that when the same actions are committed without Motivational intent, or even by a kind of Non-Life, the ethicality of the objective actions disappears either partially or entirely depending on the situation. One, do you remember how the Secondary Energy of the Self emerged from the Primary Energy of the World?

One: Yes, I do.

Two: Life is another form of Secondary Energy, and it mirrors the Energy of the Self if you look closely. Productivity mirrors Motivation, Validation mirrors Awareness, Comprehension mirrors Discernment, and ATP-Consumption mirrors Disturbances.

One: Huh… so it does. Fascinating.

Two: Now tell me… Given the revelations that you and Zero discovered over the last three days, which is more Fundamental? The Self or Life?

One: I would think that it is certainly true that the self is a subset of things endowed with the qualities of life. But at the same time, in the real world, certain life can be viewed as a subset of the self, and even the self as it is could not have emerged without other similar things existing, like parents. Either way, it follows that life is either more or equally fundamental to the self. Hey, wait, isn't this exactly the conclusion that we came to for the self being the totality of energy in the world?

Two: Correct, but they can also lead to different conclusions. One could still be all Life and still be a subset of the Energy in the World.

Zero: So life requires energy, and the self requires both life and energy. Therefore, the self is not required for either life or energy to persist, unless they are somehow equivalent. But what is odd here is that this is the opposite reasoning we used to equate energy to the dimensions that comprise it. I mean, think about it! Energy requires its parts, and each of the parts requires the totality of energy to distinguish any part at all. Yet, here we are, One! Saying the self, which is certainly a part of life and energy, is not required by energy to endure. What gives?!

One: I think it's a false equivocation fallacy. In the first instance, the energy of the world is defined by the dimensions that comprise its being. But in the second instance, the secondary energy of life in the self is only partially defined by its primary energy, and you can see how primary energy did not require life or the self to define or comprise its being. The fact that we did define these different forms of energy was a luxury, not a requirement. The freedom to define energy incorrectly by having it require the self to be complete is also a luxury of our motivation to do so.

Zero: Ah, I see now.

Two: Now back to ethics…

One: Actually, Two, I am also getting hungry. May we start heading to town to get some lunch?

Two: Good thinking, and I can relay the Truth in full once we get there. Congrats on your victory today, Zero.

One: But I don't understand why I lost yet! At least, not entirely. Why can't it be that the promotion or depreciation of the livelihood for all the objective avatars and subjects involved in an action leads to an objective moral claim? Plus, remember the rising sun foreshadowing my victory? What gives?!

Zero: Sometimes a rising sun is just a rising sun, and it doesn't mean anything extra. I'm sure Two will clarify over lunch why I won today.

The Truth

Contrary to the title of this book, there were a total of *Four Voices* that the reader could concern themselves with in this book. The clear solitary voice of the author is found here at the end of our book's journey and at the beginning in the Introduction. He is the underlying reasoning beneath these peculiar concept spaces used to explore various phenomena that concern him as a critical thinker. Hi, how are you, reader? I haven't spoken for a while, and I've been waiting to say this thing for pages upon pages. So, do you remember the 3-man chess scenario that Two declared as inevitable? Well, that part is true, it is inevitable, but I did initially simulate the whole game in my mind, and I almost had it right the first time all in my head. I drew a map long after the fact of writing the game down, just to make sure I got it right, and thank Zilch I did. But the only two goofs I made were, for one, I lost track of Two's bishop's location, which didn't significantly affect anything. And after a long rant by Two, I ended up moving Zero's pieces twice in a row. Oddly enough, the final book's game ended up a whole round quicker than the rough draft, after that. Tim isn't omniscient, *who would-a thunk it?*

Another thing I wanted to hold off saying until here, is an elaboration on Two saying that Vacuum Energy is Nothing's First Layer of Energy. In reality, sure, it *could* be viewed this way, but one, it isn't actually Energy per se, and two, I'm not using the phrase in a scientific sense, and I wanted to make that clear here. The scientific usage of vacuum energy is more of a descriptor of the subsistence of Space-Time when it's devoid of matter locally.

It's pretty much a part of the real World's infrastructure, and it has a constant non-zero value to it, which again, is not Nothing. A True and Perfect Vacuum's Energy *would* have a value of zero, and this lies only beyond the real World, which is why I'm fine leaving Two describing Nothing's Energy as Vacuum Energy, since the words used are correct, even though the scientific *meaning* underlying the words are in error. *It's not my fault scientists use so many good words and phrases that can be connected by Nothing!*

Then, for the other 3 of the 4 voices, there are Zero and One, which represent my rational and creative attributes. Psychologically, what is going on between these *Two Voices* is both a common and a relatively unique occurrence. It is common, because unlike what I said in the Introduction, about being uncertain if everybody has a Zero in their minds, the truth is, that everybody has a Zero and a One in the real world. They are the yin and yang, the light and the dark, the anima and the animus, and the calculating and the abstract. A Zero without a One would surely lead to a complete self-negation, either philosophically, by suicide, or both. There would be no light to see, and thus no world, other, or self to live for, so they would just fade into blackness. A One without a Zero would be annoying and in error *constantly.* Happy and carefree, their productions would be done without concern for safety or double-checking things, that if One was left alone to their own devices, their death would be swift if Zero never cared to stop them. Thus, the essence of war between these forces is common.

The uniqueness comes in when you consider both the outcome and the modes of interaction encountered between these two characters. In most people, there tends to be a preference for either one or the other, as in, their anima regularly overpowers and suppresses their animus into the realm of the subconscious, or vice versa. When you are the dark, and you identify with it, you fear the light. When you are the light, and you identify with it, you shine into it and find Nothing there, because all is light! But when you incorporate both and are aware of both, the strongest self will seek to keep their inner dichotomy in Equilibrium with each Other-Self. There are a plethora of references that come to mind after writing that. The common phrase "I cannot live with myself!" is a function of the stronger and more aware self being annoyed by the actions of the weaker and more subconscious self. And "bringing the balance to the Force" in *Star Wars* was never about the total domination of the Jedi over the Sith or the rule of the Empire over the Rebels. It was about the selves, portrayed as the Skywalker's, recognizing the Disequilibrium of power between the Collective anima and animus and simply placing themselves in the optimum position to create an equal balance between the *Two Forces*. I could go on, but I believe the point has been made. Unambiguous inner peace and cooperation within the self is uncommon, I think. The command or striving for peace is either dictated by the other by a sort of forced Equilibrium, let go of entirely to let it happen naturally, or endured with varying interpretations of stress.

Anywho, the fourth voice was an interesting and unplanned aspect of the creative process on my end. Two is a catch-all for my ego, my superego, God, a superior Being, an authority, and the Other who should be feared and respected. For me, what was odd about Two, is that when I was writing as him, these brilliant connections were made that seemed to come out of Nowhere. For example, when Zero is shocked into silence, and confirms with slower, more careful reasoning whatever Two just said, I was the one who was the most shocked. Two, I believe, was also a direct manifestation of my subconscious discernments bringing useful wisdom to my (and now your) awareness. Although I do not believe that personal experience is a good means of validating the Truth of the matter, to me, this experience I had with the character of Two could be used as evidence to confirm that awareness and discernment operate under separate processes in the self. More specifically, and for example, although the individual neurons that represented the 4 aspects of the self and the 4 aspects of life already existed in my brain, as things I was already aware of, the discernment used to demonstrate how exactly they mirrored each other was *not* a conscious process. I did consciously posit the question if they connected in some way or not, but the solution itself was practically flowing out of my pen *several real world days* after my awareness had given up on the problem entirely.

Should I be concerned about handing over control to my subconscious processes? Minimally. I would caution others who are less conscientious, as well as those who would attribute these subconscious revelations and drives to the divine and the demonic, respectively. But since I am aware of myself, and my disturbances are minimal, so long as I continue to try to understand my motivations, I don't need to fear them. I, as One and Zero, am capable of overthrowing myself, as Two, if my subconscious gets out of hand. If One and Zero agree that Two's rule has to end, the odds of a successful mutiny are too great (more than 50%) for Two to "act out" in the first place. Not to mention the many Ones and Zeros of others who would inevitably subjugate the avatar housing Two, that any will to power driven by Two would lead to catastrophic and equally inevitable failure in the real world.

I should also mention that a lot of the hubris portrayed in this book is very tongue-in-cheek, and I may have laid it on a little too thick. Between Zero being a more personable representation of me being a Master Negator, One being a knight in shining armor, calling myself as Two "Lord," and sometimes being too agreeable with myself, all put together looks like a 3-way daisy chain with myself at times. There's a fine line between self-confidence and cocky self-delusion, and as a creator, I'm comfortable going wherever it is most entertaining and engaging to the reader. Of course, I say this in a book that had the bore of a dictionary in a couple of places due to the minor alterations of the definitions, but my reason for leaving those boring segments in the final book is an extension of the part of the hubris that is genuine. If anything, this book can be made as a snippet of my thought processes, and in the event any current or future scholars care enough about *how* I thought, in addition to *what* I thought, this text could be of notable use to them in that regard.

Beyond this, the Truth behind *Two Voices* has been the pursuit of it. I am aware that *Four Voices* may have been the more accurate title, but only One and Zero, as I conversed with myself, were necessary to bring the Truth out, as best as I can say. I who am currently speaking is One and Zero speaking simultaneously, as the full extent of my current awareness has reached a consensus on what I deem to be the Truth. And Two, again, is more of a projection of myself, the total iceberg, if you will, that I use to allow myself to bring truth from the subconscious in an attempt to increase what I am aware of. To be honest, I hate to be capitalizing the T in Truth in this final section, as it implies its absoluteness and irrefutability. It implies that there will never be a need for revision or translation, since the Truth will remain True no matter the Time or Space it is proclaimed.

The Truth is that no Truth is self-evident or irrefutable seeing that many others are either complete idiots or witty geniuses who could refute the roundness of a circle, given the chance. But in this book, as well as my other literary works, the Truth is whatever remains after my Zero throws his best at a proposition, and something substantial remains. It doesn't mean that superior evidence or reasoning doesn't exist, but that by the standards of my reasoning, which I'm improving every day I live, I am currently unable to refute or revise the Truths contained herein.

So here, in summary, are the Truths discovered and proclaimed in this book, for future reference for mySelf and Others in a future Time in the real World of concern.

1) A **World** is *the totality of its Mass-Electric-Space-Time Energy.*

2) From these 4 Primary Dimensions, all objective phenomena can be measured with the aid of *a systemic equivocation of units,* which I call **Quanta**.

3) **Space** is *the totality of distances to other points of contact.*

4) **Time** is *the totality of endurance for a point of contact.*

5) **Electric** is *the totality of sensible appearances concerning points of contact.*

6) **Mass** is *the totality of physical resistance to changes of action.*

7) **Energy** is *Mass and/or Light, either enduring or moving through Space-Time.*

As an elaboration, Vacuum Energy can only be observed as a sensible appearance in a World, so even when a controlled section of Space-Time holds the amount of 0 Mass and 0 Electromagnetic phenomena, it cannot negate the Mass-Electric Dimensions/fields in-themselves within a World. Therefore, as I defined it, the Mass-Electric fields must always endure, and simply removing all substances, which are units of interactive Energy, does not and cannot negate a minimum amount of potential Energy within an observable World for a Non-Zero amount of substance to move through it.

8) A **Self** is *a unit of Energy with the capacity to be Aware of, Discerning of, Motivated by, and Disturbed by the World of concern and itSelf.*

9) From a Self arises **Qualia**, which is *the total subjective Dimensional analysis of things.*

10) A **thing** is *a unit of Energy, and the total subjective Dimensional analysis of the unit.*

As an elaboration, Nothing holds 0 units of Energy of concern, and since the subjective Dimensional analysis of 0 units of Energy can never be observed in an observable World, the Qualia of Nothing is Non-applicable. By contrast, Everything holds and is equivalent to the totality of Energy of concern, and since different units within the totality of Energy of concern hold the potential to hold variable units of Qualia between themselves both from the perspective of the Self and Others, the Qualia of Everything of concern should be limited in its utility.

Within a Self, there are 4 Fundamental Aspects, which will now be defined in further detail.

11) **Awareness** is *the capacity for accurate perceptions within the World of concern and itSelf.*

12) **Discernment** is *the capacity for accurate and/or ethical judgments of actions within the World of concern and itSelf.*

13) **Motivation** is *the capacity to desire and/or avoid actions and/or things within the World of concern and itSelf.*

14) (Self) **Disturbance** is *the capacity to be mentally troubled and/or distracted by the World of concern and itSelf.*

As a general elaboration, when I was speaking as Zero on the Self, I genuinely thought Self-negation was the correct philosophy, thinking One didn't stand a chance on the 2nd Day at the start of my writing Day 2. I was pleasantly surprised to prove Zero's idea wrong. I am what I am Aware of. To even think Self-negation was possible whilst remaining alive was a process of flawed Discernment. I, and Others, are defined by the actions they are Motivated towards accomplishing in the future and accomplished in the past. I am Motivated to be mySelf, and maintain and improve my own and my wife's Livelihood, and Others beyond us as far as we are capable of helping. I am Motivated to write down my ideas and share them with Others in the World to perhaps increase their Livelihood as well. I am now an author thanks to my past Motivations. Also, to be Motivated to love Others, I believe, implies that there is a Self in the Life forms with Awareness and Discernment to a degree capable of receiving the Motivated effort put into them. Non-Life receiving love is not love, but maintenance.

This active changing of my mind is reflected in the style of this book, as a sort of stream-of-consciousness that went into often chaotic and abrupt shifts in content and tone. If any of the pedantries of definition-seeking induced boredom to you at any point, I do apologize. The benefit should be viewed as the level of care that I put into the words and definitions I use when I use them. To remove the Self would be to remove subjectivity, and the words attributed to the Qualia of things would be describing Nothing to Nobody who would be capable of comprehending the meaning of the words. Like, seriously, your Awareness of these words typed before you give these words meaning. You turn them from ink Energy on paper Energy, into distinguishable and meaningful Other things that are not the First Layer of Energy contained in the book before you. So to those Selves who endured the controlled chaos with me by reading this far, thank you for adding your personal Second Layer of Energy to my words, no matter how far misunderstood or weak you perceive my words are to begin with.

Zero: Man, this barbecue looks good! It appears to brighten my whole perspective! The gray background of my world's appearance is being painted a shimmering brown!
Two: Ha Ha! No Zero, you just got sauce all over your eyes!
One: Do you need a napkin?

Zero: No, thanks, I feel so happy! Everything is so beautiful right now, a sweet victory, a sweet sauce, and a couple of sweet friends! I'll wash up after we're done here.

One: If you say so… So Two, how did I lose today?

Two: You still haven't figured it out after all this Time? Eat your brisket, and hear the words of Two! I am the omniscient arbiter of morals, so you better listen well! Now tell me, One, as the highest authority over yourSelf, Discern for me, and answer me this simple question. *Do I have a Self?*

One: Of course you do, my Lord! Your words are filled with life, truth, and meaning! How could you not have a self?

Zero: Well, you see…

Two: Silence, Zero! Not now, not while these words are surely here before the readers! For now, let One's assessment remain True for the sake of argument. For One is correct, I do have a Self. Morals are given from my Discernment and are then delegated to the rest of my kingdom. Therefore, One, your morality is based upon my subject/mySelf/my Discernment, is it not?

One: In this concept space, sure, I understand that. But did we not also determine that the secondary layer of energy of the self and life directly stems from the objective first layer of energy in the real world?

Zero: Yes, but the only real way to verify the ethicalness' objectivity would be to then connect it directly to the world's energy, and demonstrate how that configuration or actions of energy is inherently evil in-itself.

Two: Correct. And I can hear your thoughts, One. You were wondering if the darkness of Mass and entropy's manifestation of Disturbance in Time are the objective sources of evil, and the Electric's Light and the vastness of Space are the objective sources of good. This is not the case, for although Light is vital for Life, too much Light can be detrimental to One's Livelihood. Although the pure Mass of a black hole can be detrimental to Life, from a safe distance in Space, they can prove to be vital for the formation of galaxies capable of supporting Life.

One: Aye, you're right… the energy dimensions cannot always be good or evil… especially if they need to be together to form a world to house the self discerning the morality in the first place.

Two: And yet, you still wonder if a certain configuration of Energy could demonstrate itSelf to be always evil. And I'm telling you, no, it cannot.

One: Why?

Zero: Omnomnom, because then non-living objects would then be able to either always affirm or negate life.

One: But time *does* always negate life!

Two: Yet, it never could have begun without it. Thus, whenever it is observed by a Self in Time in the World's Energy, Time is seen to always affirm Life as well.

One: Hmmm… I see.

Two: Both good and evil require Energy to be Validated as such. Yet, no configuration or part of Energy can be observed as purely One or the Other.

One: But if pure goodness and pure evil cannot be traced back to its energy, *from whence cometh evil?*

Zero: Omnomnom, from a self, you dingus! Why did you think I tried affirming self-negation yesterday, for the giggles? No, it was to try to rid the evil aspects of my self from myself.

Two: But you didn't realize that doing so would also rid the good aspects of yourSelf.

One: I see. A judgment cannot be made without a subjective self to be disturbed by evil and motivated towards good and/or evil. To discern and be aware of evil, one needs only a self.

Two: Correct, but the same goes for goodness as well. They are both contained in the Self. And it is up to the Self how they choose to cultivate said goodness or evil within. And it is up to the Selves within the Collective to Discern what laws should be implemented to subjugate certain evils from being detrimental to the Collective's Livelihood.

One: I… Hmmm… I agree? So I concede fully, Zero. You win today.

Zero: Have some ribs, One. It's ok to taste the spoils of my sweet victory. I consider this a win for all of us.

Two: Indeed, the pathway beyond good and evil may not be the most clear to travel, but it is the correct path. I am sure of it. It is clear from my perspective.

Zero: Omnomnom, I dare not negate those words, your Highness!

So, allow me the courtesy to make the Truth clear, or at least as clear as I am capable of. The Truth underlying ethics is oftentimes determined by those in power to enforce their individual standards. So long as those standards lead to consistent consequences in the real World, it would be alright to consider such laws objective, even whilst being originated by subjects, however, it is not necessary for the laws to be effective as such. Although the words used to define unlawful actions hold no objective inherent meaning, the consensus of meaning between a multitude of subjects can still nevertheless be transcendental to the Collective, and can bring meaning to the core of the Life-Energy that unites the Collective with the Self. In this way, not all lawful actions are ethical, and not all ethical actions are lawful. Whenever the net Life-Energy of the Collective is diminishable by a certain law, the ethical thing to do would be to stand against that law to promote change in a manner consistent with justice and with appropriate force.

15) Now, concerning Life, **Comprehension** is *the ability to learn and distinguish things in the World of concern.*

16) **ATP-Consumption** is *the ability to use adenosine triphosphate as an avatar's primary source of Energy at a cellular level.*

17) **Production** is *the ability to maintain the avatar's well-being by moving things into more useful positions and actions for itSelf.*

18) **Validation** is *the ability to confirm itSelf to be Life in the Self and Others by enduring Disturbances and other trials in the World.*

19) If a thing can demonstrate to hold all 4 of those Fundamental Aspects of Life, it is certainly Life.

20) If a thing holds only 3 of these Fundamental Aspects of Life and fails to demonstrate itSelf on the 4th, it shall still be considered as Life.

21) If a thing holds only 1 of these Fundamental Aspects of Life, such as AI's Comprehension, a virus'

ATP-Consumption, a simple robot's Production, or God's Validation, it shall be considered as Non-Life as if it held 0 of these.

22) If a thing can demonstrate half of these Fundamental Aspects of Life, if it includes Validation, it is Non-Life.

23) But if a thing holds either Comprehension & ATP-Consumption, Comprehension & Production, or ATP-Consumption & Production, *it is debatable* and can depend on a case-by-case basis and to the degrees these Fundamental Aspects manifest themselves.

24) For the betterment of all Life in the World of concern, to increase the Livelihood of Life and to increase each Life in question's capacity for Life in their Energy/Selves is ethical.

25) All hindrances and deductions of Livelihood, by contrast, are debatable concerning their ethicality on a case-by-case basis, even though the appearances of depreciation appear to generally be unethical.

Life, in general, is good, and Non-Life is neither good nor evil, even if it appears to be evil in most cases from Life's perspective.

26) Therefore, the optimum way to fight evil is by simply promoting the general Livelihood to ourSelves and Others

whenever they likewise promote the general Livelihood in the real World of concern.

27) The **reader** is about to enter *The Great Nothingness that comes After this book.* Surely, there are more things that will come after this book, but THIS book is done, and there is nothing more to say. Finito. It is finished; you can stop reading now. Stop it. Just let it end, Zilch damn it. Oh shit, was that my first time throwing out expletives in this book? Ctrl+F… Yup, it sure was. This is a True thing, yup yup yup. *A very important Truth.* The Non-sense has continued, but the book is finished. I should just make a comedy book, I bet that would slap some knees. Here I am, writing that the Truth is Absurd, because it is relative to what it is describing. If you got to this point, good job, you can read. Congratulations. You get a cookie. *A Concept Space Cookie.* SPACE COOKIES, THAT SOUNDS OUT OF THIS WORLD! *Hold up, space cookies have marijuana in them?* THAT'S A GREAT IDEA FOR A BOOK, I'M GONNA WRITE A BOOK COMPLETELY HIGH ON SPACE COOKIES! *(Or edibles, heh.)*